Improving Outcomes with Clinical Decision Support: An Implementer's Guide

Jerome A. Osheroff, MD, FACP, FACMI
Eric A. Pifer, MD
Jonathan M. Teich, MD, PhD, FACMI
Dean F. Sittig, PhD, FACMI
Robert A. Jenders, MD, MS, FACP

Supported in part by a generous grant
from Thomson Micromedex.

HIMSS Mission

To lead change in the healthcare information and management systems field through knowledge sharing, advocacy, collaboration, innovation, and community affiliations.

Contents

About the Authors

Jerome A. Osheroff, MD, FACP, FACMI, is Chief Clinical Informatics Officer at Thomson Micromedex, where he helps ensure that the company's current and future clinical decision support offerings are optimally responsive to healthcare needs. For two decades Dr. Osheroff has been building understanding of clinicians' information needs and helping ensure that information technology is successfully applied to fulfilling these needs better. These efforts include guiding development of commercially successful clinical decision support products, helping healthcare organizations and clinicians use CDS to improve care processes and outcomes, leading research into clinical information management, and helping guide national policy on CDS. Dr. Osheroff is on the medical staff and is Adjunct Assistant Professor of Medicine at the University of Pennsylvania Health System in Philadelphia. He is a fellow of the American College of Physicians and the American College of Medical Informatics and chairs the HIMSS Clinical Decision Support Task Force.

Eric A. Pifer, MD, is Assistant Professor of Medicine and Chief Medical Informatics Officer at the University of Pennsylvania Health System (UPHS) in Philadelphia, where he has led the implementation and customization of clinical information systems since 1998. He has done this through clear articulation of the value of information systems in improving healthcare, the creation of a strategic vision, and the active management of a team of professionals devoted to this process. Dr. Pifer remains active in internal medicine practice and clinical teaching while maintaining a primary professional focus on deploying clinical decision support interventions to improve the quality of care for patients at UPHS.

Jonathan M. Teich, MD, PhD, FACMI, is a co-founder, Senior Vice President, and Chief Medical Officer of Healthvision in Waltham, Massachusetts. He is also Assistant Professor of Medicine at Harvard University and is a practicing emergency physician at Brigham and Women's Hospital in Boston. Before joining Healthvision, he led the design of the advanced clinical systems at Brigham and Women's and at Partners Healthcare, including CPOE, ambulatory medical records, emergency medicine systems, and information resources for patients, all with emphasis on clinical decision support. Dr. Teich's main focus has been the use of information systems to directly improve care, prevent adverse events, streamline clinical workflow and access to services, and help guide health decisions. Dr. Teich has authored over 90 publications in the field of medical informatics. He is a board member of the eHealth Initiative Foundation, a fellow of the American College of Medical Informatics, and chair of the HIMSS Patient Safety and Quality Committee.

Dean F. Sittig, PhD, FACMI, is the Director of Applied Research in Medical Informatics for Northwest Permanente, the physician's group practice associated with the Kaiser Permanente Hospitals and Health Plan. He also serves as an Adjunct Associate Professor of Medical Informatics and Clinical Epidemiology at the Oregon Health and Science University in Portland, Oregon. Dr. Sittig's research interests center on the design, development, implementation, and evaluation of all aspects of clinical information systems with a special emphasis on clinical decision support. Dr. Sittig is the founding editor of *The Informatics Review,* an online serial devoted to helping clinicians and information technology professionals keep up-to-date with the rapidly advancing field of medical informatics. Finally,

Dr. Sittig is a founding member of the Improve-IT Institute, a collaborative research initiative that attempts to provide the evidence that increased information technology capabilities, availability, and use leads directly to improved clinical quality, safety, and effectiveness.

Robert A. Jenders, MD, MS, FACP, is Associate Professor of Clinical Medicine at Cedars-Sinai Medical Center (CSMC) and the University of California, Los Angeles (UCLA). He is also Co-Chair of the Clinical Decision Support Technical Committee of Health Level 7 (HL-7). For the past decade, Dr. Jenders has worked in clinical informatics, teaching in informatics graduate education programs, conducting research and development in clinical decision support systems, and lecturing at international meetings. In addition, for the past eight years he has worked principally in HL-7 and with other organizations, such as the California Healthcare Foundation and the National Immunization Program of the U.S. Centers for Disease Control and Prevention, to develop standards and promote their use in healthcare computing. In addition to teaching internal medicine and medical informatics at CSMC and UCLA, Dr. Jenders applies this experience to the development of decision support systems and electronic health records at Cedars-Sinai Medical Center.

Preface

Much of the sustained enthusiasm and support for health information technology during the past several years stems from landmark reports in the 1990s demonstrating the ability of such technology to prevent errors, reduce adverse events, and improve the quality of care. In almost all of those landmark studies, the gains came directly from the application of clinical decision support (CDS) interventions—reminders, alerts, constrained choices, tailored forms, just-in-time references, and more—to common medical processes. In the trend-setting Institute of Medicine (IOM) reports, *To Err Is Human* and *Crossing the Quality Chasm*, CDS was endorsed as one of the most powerful tools available in the national quest toward improved patient safety and healthcare quality.

The premise is correct: new studies demonstrating the positive impact of CDS continue to appear in the literature. However, its impact on a national scale has been muted to date, with a resulting delay in some of those expected major improvements. Implementation of CDS in hospitals, practices, home care, and other settings proceeds slowly, with great difficulty, and with more than a few bumps in the road. Without a common framework from which to work, each organization must discover for itself the key steps needed to gather the right stakeholders together, to find CDS interventions that are acceptable and effective, to manage their testing and implementation, and to demonstrate their positive impact.

At the same time, developers and vendors of CDS-bearing applications, such as clinical knowledge bases and computerized provider order entry (CPOE) systems, re-invent their own particular wheel, each one trying to produce effective interventions and presentation formats from a mixture of personal experience, anecdotes in the literature,

and empirical guesses. Without a shared body of knowledge, practical lessons learned in one setting are difficult to apply elsewhere. Both the production of CDS systems and their implementation are, in many ways, hit-or-miss processes, with failure still a distinct possibility. Recent reports about "unintended consequences" of healthcare information technology further highlight the urgent need to get CDS implementation right the first time, every time.

This book is intended as a response to this need. The authors have seen these processes and pitfalls repeated many times over—sometimes many times over at a single institution. We began working together on this project in the winter of 2003 as friends and colleagues who had many decades of collective experience working to improve healthcare outcomes through CDS interventions. This experience reflects a variety of different perspectives, including those of healthcare providers and delivery organizations, vendors of clinical information systems and clinical knowledge content, standards organizations, and academic medical informatics laboratories. Our goal was, and remains, to create a focal point for distilling the collective wisdom about successful CDS implementation into practically useful guidance. We were pleased to join forces on this effort with the Healthcare Information and Management Systems Society (HIMSS), which has devoted its own considerable talent and resources to supporting and facilitating the project. It is our hope that by collecting best practices and key lessons, building a common framework, and putting it all into a step-by-step guide, we will be helping you to avoid common mistakes and to create highly effective CDS, smoothly and efficiently. We also hope that the framework and classifications in this guide will become a basis for sharing research and experience about CDS successes and failures, so that lessons learned at one organization can be used by others without having to repeat the same experiments.

We are pleased at the response to the first edition, known as the *Clinical Decision Support Implementer's Workbook*, which was published in 2004. Many readers have told us that they have followed that guide closely as a user's manual for their own CDS programs and projects; others have appreciated the single-book compilation of lessons and strategies covering the entire CDS project cycle. In this second edition, re-titled *Improving Outcomes with Clinical Decision Support: An Implementer's Guide*, we have made a major effort to strengthen the usability and value of the book as a practical guide for CDS implementers, and as an important resource for system developers and CDS researchers as well. In particular, this edition adds detailed examples throughout to illustrate the use of the worksheets and forms, and much more on the categorization and practical use of objective classes and interventions, which are key concepts in selecting the best intervention for a given situation. Many new topics requested by readers have been addressed, including governance and management for CDS programs, knowledge management, cost justification, and ensuring that anticipated benefits are realized.

None of the words in this book would have appeared in print without the help of many persons besides the authors listed on the cover. In particular, we want to acknowledge the deep contributions of our teammates at HIMSS—Gail Arnett, Pat Wise, and Fran Perveiler, and our chief editor, Mary Kelly. They have provided support, know-how, experience, and just plain hard work to make this vision come alive. We would like to acknowledge Michael Chase, Jim Cimino, Tonya Hongsermeier, Alan Peres, Kirk Rasmussen, Cali Samuels, and Doug Thompson for helping develop some of the key ideas in this edition of the book. We would also like to acknowledge the thoughtful review and helpful input of Joseph Ketcherside, Hyung T. Kim, Manlik Kwong, Gil Kuperman, Robert Murphy, Tom Payne, and Andy Steele. We also, of course, gratefully appreciate the support of our families, co-workers, and employers, who supported us as we devoted many hours to this work.

In addition, we are grateful to all of the readers who wrote in with helpful comments, suggestions, and proposed additions. We have tried to incorporate many of those suggestions in the current work, and we encourage you to continue to send feedback and ideas that can be incorporated into future revisions. For us, this book is not a finished work; rather, it is a springboard into a number of other activities designed to help CDS fulfill its original promise: to be a vitally important, routinely used tool that helps bring the best care to the largest number of patients. We hope you will continue to be our partners in that journey.

JO, EP, JT, DS, RJ
2005

Introduction

Healthcare has lagged behind many other industries in applying information systems to improve processes and outcomes, and there is intense global interest in closing this gap. Major national efforts are underway to promote more widespread and effective use of tools such as the **electronic medical record (EMR)** and **computerized provider order entry (CPOE)** to address these problems. Much of the implementation activity in the United States, for example, focuses on dissemination and initial adoption of these systems. Although computerizing clinical data and transactions can substantially improve information management in patient care, this automation reaches its full potential only when pertinent clinical knowledge is combined with the data to inform care decisions and actions.

Providing pertinent knowledge within workflow to inform care is a challenge for most healthcare organizations, particularly when that workflow involves **clinical information systems (CIS)**. This book is designed as a practical tool intended to help healthcare institutions deliver this knowledge, or **clinical decision support (CDS),** in ways that measurably improve outcomes important to the organization. It does this by guiding the planning, development, implementation, and evaluation of **CDS interventions** that will effectively address specific clinical or strategic concerns.

Improving Outcomes with Clinical Decision Support: An Implementer's Guide first helps organizations identify stakeholders in their CDS programs. It then guides them through the steps of working with these **stakeholders** to

- Determine the **CDS program's goals and clinical objectives;**
- Catalog local information systems capabilities to help achieve those **targets;**
- Select the best approach to address the targets with specific **CDS interventions;**
- Develop the interventions;
- Make sure those interventions are acceptable to stakeholders and put them into use; and
- Monitor and enhance the CDS program on an ongoing basis to ensure it achieves the desired organizational objectives.

AUDIENCE

This book is designed to help healthcare organizations build a comprehensive and systematic approach to addressing organizational needs through a CDS program. It is also designed to help with the development and implementation of specific CDS interventions that may be part of such a program. Organizations with applications in place that support robust CDS interventions, such as CPOE or an EMR, will have a greater range of CDS options to consider in developing the program. Organizations with more limited clinical information systems currently in place will also find valuable strategies for more fully leveraging their infrastructure and for planning for enhanced CDS as more sophisticated systems are implemented.

Individuals who are responsible for developing and implementing an organization's CDS strategy, and those who have a leadership role in improving patient safety and quality, will benefit from this book. They may have broad leadership roles, such as chief medical/nursing/quality/safety officers. They may also

- Be leaders in key quality-related departments such as pharmacy and laboratory;
- Hold information systems positions such as chief information officer or clinical director of information systems; or

Definitions

Different readers might have different ideas about the meaning of many of the central terms used throughout this book. To help ensure clarity and consistency, we define our use of these terms in the glossary at the end of this book. Glossary terms are boldfaced the first time they are used in the text. Several of the most critical definitions are also presented below.

- **Clinical decision support (CDS)** refers broadly to providing clinicians or patients with clinical knowledge and patient-related information, intelligently filtered, or presented at appropriate times, to enhance patient care. Clinical knowledge of interest could include simple facts and relationships, established best practices for managing patients with specific disease states, new medical knowledge from clinical research, and many other types of information (see Figure 2-5, page 33).
- **High-level CDS goals** are high-level or strategic targets, such as increasing patient safety, that an organization might address with CDS (see Figure 1-5, page 7).
- **Clinical goals** are more specific than CDS goals and include desired care processes or outcomes, such as reducing complications from diabetic kidney disease (see Figure 1-5).

- **Clinical objectives** are more specific and measurable components of clinical goals, such as increasing the rate of appropriate screening for diabetic kidney disease (see Figure 1-5).
- A **CDS intervention** involves delivering one or more specific pieces of clinical information (knowledge and/or data) to an individual, at a specific time and place, to address a clinical objective. CDS interventions include the CDS content and the method for delivering that content (e.g., which software application, which type of presentation, or where in the workflow process). A simple rule-based **alert,** such as a drug allergy warning, is one of the most recognizable types of CDS intervention; however, as illustrated in Figure 2-5, page 33, the range of CDS interventions is broad and extends far beyond rule-based approaches. While there are many successful examples of CDS provided via paper-based systems, this book focuses on computer-facilitated interventions.
- A **CDS program** consists of the overall set of CDS interventions that an organization uses to achieve its healthcare goals, as well as the processes used to select, prioritize, implement and evaluate these

- Participate in departmental or organization-wide safety and quality programs.

In organizations not yet ready to embark on a comprehensive CDS program, individuals in these positions can use this book to help implement more limited and focused CDS interventions, and potentially help educate the organization about the value of a broader approach as well. CDS system develop-

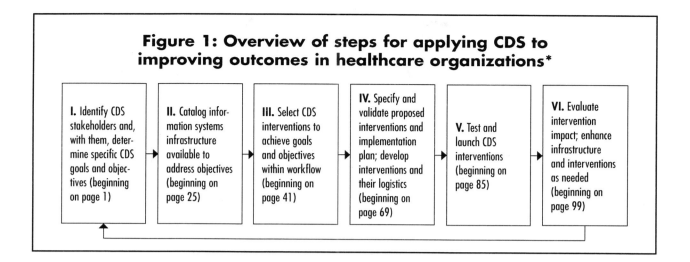

Figure 1: Overview of steps for applying CDS to improving outcomes in healthcare organizations*

I. Identify CDS stakeholders and, with them, determine specific CDS goals and objectives (beginning on page 1)

II. Catalog information systems infrastructure available to address objectives (beginning on page 25)

III. Select CDS interventions to achieve goals and objectives within workflow (beginning on page 41)

IV. Specify and validate proposed interventions and implementation plan; develop interventions and their logistics (beginning on page 69)

V. Test and launch CDS interventions (beginning on page 85)

VI. Evaluate intervention impact; enhance infrastructure and interventions as needed (beginning on page 99)

ers and researchers may also find the framework and material in the book useful.

USING THIS BOOK

This book's approach to CDS implementation involves a series of major steps or processes, outlined above and schematically in Figure 1. Each chapter is designed to provide a substantial educational background on the major issues and also to walk the reader step-by-step through the necessary tasks to complete the process successfully in a real clinical environment. Each chapter includes

- An overview of the tasks;
- A summary of key lessons;
- A discussion of pertinent issues;
- Worksheets (with sample data) and recommendations to help gather, organize, and process institution-specific information critical to accomplishing the tasks;
- Concluding comments; and
- A bibliography with references and Web links to additional readings and resources.

The online book supplement (www.himss.org/cdsguide) is a companion resource. It contains blank

templates for each worksheet that readers can download and use in their own organizations.

This book helps focus, enhance, and organize your approach to CDS planning and implementation. Although the guidance builds successively with each chapter, it is not essential to work through the book in a strictly linear fashion, to address every step, or to complete each worksheet. For example, you might focus on specific sections that address issues that are important or timely in your organization. Similarly, you can use the ideas reflected in the worksheets and steps as background material to validate or stimulate your own CDS approach.

All of the authors of this book work in the U.S. When we make reference to professional and governmental organizations, we typically employ examples drawn from the U.S. However, most of the fundamental drivers and issues related to CDS implementation are not specific to any single country. The authors expect that the approach to CDS outlined in this book will be useful outside the U.S., though readers from other countries may need to consider analogous professional and governmental initiatives pertinent to their environment.

Iterative Refinement of This Book—Your Role

The first edition of this book was published in February 2004 and was well received by the CDS

---

* Figure 1 graphically depicts the clinical decision support implementation steps around which this book is organized. This is a cyclical process; results from each CDS implementation cycle feed back into subsequent iterations through each step.

implementer community as a valuable resource. Many readers offered helpful suggestions for enhancing its usefulness; some of these readers had extensive expertise in CDS implementation, while others were just starting out. This second edition incorporates a large number of those enhancements.

If you have successfully accomplished specific CDS tasks or used the first edition of this book, we are most interested in hearing about your experiences and insights. We would particularly appreciate the chance to see any sample documents, completed worksheets, and other implementation tools from your CDS program that you would be willing to share with others. We would also appreciate feedback from those just beginning to develop a CDS program. Your input will help us provide clearer and more valuable guidance to other such readers. Whatever your stage in the process, your input is welcome; we have already begun collecting ideas for the third edition! You can reach us via e-mail at cdsguide@himss.org.

Based on the widespread interest in the first edition, the **Healthcare Information and Management Systems Society (HIMSS)** has launched a CDS Task Force to help build and support the community of CDS implementers. Short-term goals include optimizing the dissemination, successful use, and enhancement of this book. A longer-term goal is to create an active forum for mutual support among the CDS implementer community. If these activities sound interesting to you, we welcome your involvement. You can send an e-mail to cdsguide@himss.org for additional information.

A Note about Internet Resources

All Internet Web links cited in this book were accessible as of April 2005.

Chapter 1

Identifying Stakeholders and Goals

To create a solid foundation for the clinical decision support (CDS) program, those responsible for its development should begin by identifying key stakeholders and working with them to establish goals and objectives. New teams and roles related to developing the CDS program and to realizing benefits from it will more than likely be required.

TASKS

1. Meet with key local committees, positions, and individuals engaged in activities pertinent to an organizational CDS initiative, and document their potential goals and objectives for the CDS program (Worksheet 1-1, page 17).

2. Synthesize and validate a unified working list of organizational goals and objectives for your CDS program. Break down each high-level goal into a set of more specific clinical goals, and then break down each clinical goal into measurable clinical objectives. Define baseline and target performance pertinent to each objective (Worksheet 1-2, page 19).

Key Lessons

- A successful CDS program emerges from, and in turn supports, key organizational **performance improvement** initiatives. Executive support for the program is vitally important.

- Program goals are determined from a thorough environmental survey of pertinent initiatives and stakeholders. A variety of external drivers and internal needs combine to drive priorities for development of CDS interventions.

- **Governance** and management structures and processes need to be established for the CDS program elements, which include intervention needs assessment, design, development, testing, **launch,** and evaluation.

- **Champions**—key supporters who are trusted by your staff—are an important resource for cultivating proper two-way communication about, and support for, the CDS program.

DISCUSSION
People: The Keys to Success

Although information systems process and deliver CDS interventions, a successful CDS program requires at least as much attention to *people* issues as it does to technology and information delivery. People determine the organizational needs and outcomes the CDS program will address and are a crucial factor in each step that determines whether or not these are achieved. Individuals must agree on specific CDS goals and objectives, and on which CDS interventions can help achieve their goals and objectives. They must support the implementation of CDS interventions, incorporate them into their **workflow,** and respond appropriately when they are delivered. These tasks can require significant behavior changes for both individuals and organizations. There is an extensive body of literature on successfully managing organizational change.[1] Reviewing these resources may prove useful in building your CDS program.

An essential first step in establishing a CDS program is identifying the key individuals, committees, and positions upon which the program's success will depend—we refer to these in this book as "stakeholders." Effectively collaborating with these constituents is critical to CDS program success, and these relationships will be emphasized throughout the steps outlined in this book. Figure 1-1 lists various committees and roles that generally participate as stakeholders in CDS programs.

As you think about stakeholders, keep in mind that these roles and committees will interact with your CDS program in the context of your organization's overall governance and management structures and processes.

CDS Program Governance and Management

Even in relatively modest CDS programs consisting of a few CDS interventions, there are important decisions to be made and processes to be managed; CDS governance and management structures are therefore required to fill these needs. For example,

who will decide what issues will be addressed with CDS interventions? What is the nature and content of the CDS interventions? Who will be responsible for developing, implementing, and maintaining the interventions, and measuring their effects? These issues are handled differently in different organizations depending on the overall approach to governance and management and how related clinical and information technology (IT) initiatives are handled. Some organizations utilize existing clinical or IT/CIS committees. Increasingly, organizations are establishing dedicated positions, committees, and departments to manage the CDS program.

In either case, developing a CDS program as outlined in this book will often involve shifts in control and stakeholder interactions for various care processes. For example, CDS interventions focused on medication safety may affect the way the pharmacy and therapeutics committee, nurses, pharmacists, physicians, and patients interact at various stages in the medication management process. Ownership of process improvement by affected stakeholders should be fostered early in the development of CDS governance and management structures, particularly for any stakeholders that might be critical of the changes.

Figure 1-2, page 4, outlines different groups of CDS stakeholders and the functions of each with respect to the organization's CDS program. Figure 1-3, page 5, illustrates how these functions inter-relate in the program's life cycle. We will refer back to these figures throughout this book since they describe, in a generic way, an organizational framework for the many activities related to a CDS program. As your CDS program unfolds, you might find it helpful to use these figures to create an organizational chart and list of stakeholder roles and interactions within the program.

CDS Program Goals, and Clinical Goals and Objectives

CDS program goals consist of strategic targets, such as improved medication safety and improved cost

Figure 1-1: Stakeholders for individual CDS interventions and overall CDS program

Committees

- ❏ Pharmacy and Therapeutics
- ❏ Quality Assurance (organizationwide)
- ❏ Quality (Departmental)
- ❏ Patient Safety
- ❏ Utilization Review (organizationwide or departmental, such as blood product use)
- ❏ Medical Staff
- ❏ Residency/training
- ❏ Clinical information systems (e.g., implementation, oversight, benefits realization)
- ❏ Guideline/Practice Standards, Clinical Strategy, Disease/Care Management
- ❏ Medical Records

Positions

- ❏ Medical Director of Clinical Decision Support
- ❏ Chief Medical Officer/Medical Director
- ❏ Chief Medical Information Officer/Medical Director of Information Systems
- ❏ Chief Information Officer
- ❏ Pharmacy Director
- ❏ VP/Director of Nursing
- ❏ Quality Officer
- ❏ Patient Safety Officer
- ❏ Risk Management Officer
- ❏ Department Chairs
- ❏ Residency/Training Directors
- ❏ IPA/Physician Group chairs
- ❏ Legal Counsel

Other CDS stakeholders

- ❏ Clinicians vocal on clinical computing/CDS issues (positively or negatively)
- ❏ Clinical thought leaders
- ❏ Patients/patient representatives

effectiveness of care, which the organization plans to address with CDS interventions. The process outlined in this book emphasizes maintaining a tight link between organizational priorities and the CDS program's interventions and results. Many businesses use management systems that link high-level

Figure 1-2: Generic outline of CDS program stakeholder groups and responsibilities

Executive leadership: sets strategy, clinical standards, allocates resources

Management/Oversight
- **Healthcare organization departments/functions:** responsible for processes/outcomes that will be affected by CDS program
  - **Clinical departments (e.g., laboratory, pharmacy, medicine, surgery)**
  - **Organized medical staff**
  - **Cross-cutting functions (e.g., quality, safety, disease management)**
  - **Clinical director of information systems/medical informatics**
  - **Other organizational committees and departments**
- **CDS oversight/Benefits realization:** provides guidance/review of CDS initiatives
- **CIO/IT steering:** responsible for IT infrastructure for CDS

Implementation/Project management: develops, deploys, monitors CDS interventions
- CDS-specific: overall responsibility to deploy/maintain CDS knowledge assets
- General IT: overall responsibility to deploy/maintain clinical information systems

End-users and related positions
- End-users: recipients of CDS interventions (e.g., patients, nurses, pharmacists, physicians)
- Related staff: generate data for, or are affected by, interventions
- Subject matter experts: clinical authorities for content in CDS interventions
- Clinical thought leaders and champions (i.e., clinicians respected and listened to by colleagues): promote dissemination

goals to specific performance objectives and process outcomes.[2] These approaches will likely find wider application in patient care delivery as health system reimbursement is increasingly tied to clinical performance. CDS program goals will emerge from the interplay of external drivers and internal priorities and needs.

External Drivers
Quality Measures and Pay-for-Performance Programs
An important healthcare marketplace trend to consider as a backdrop for CDS programs is the emergence of pay-for-performance initiatives that more tightly couple provider reimbursement to measurable value in the process and outcomes of care. Those who pay for care, including employers, health plans, and the federal government, have set up dozens of these programs, and many millions of dollars of performance-linked compensation have already been paid to physicians and hospitals.[3]

Pay-for-performance and related clinical quality improvement initiatives rely on quality measures. These measures address the extent to which healthcare services shown to improve outcomes are actually being delivered to patients for whom they are indicated. For example, both the **Joint Commission on Accreditation of Healthcare Organizations**

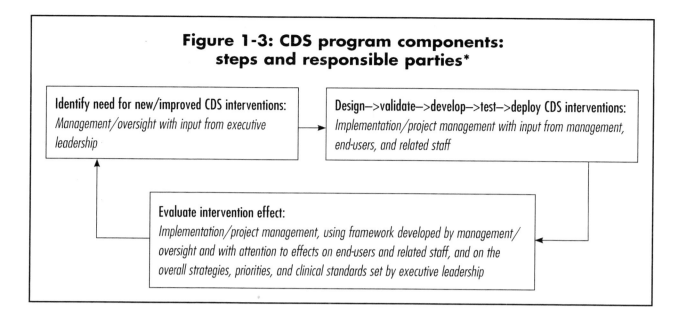

Figure 1-3: CDS program components: steps and responsible parties*

Identify need for new/improved CDS interventions: *Management/oversight with input from executive leadership*

Design–>validate–>develop–>test–>deploy CDS interventions: *Implementation/project management with input from management, end-users, and related staff*

Evaluate intervention effect: *Implementation/project management, using framework developed by management/oversight and with attention to effects on end-users and related staff, and on the overall strategies, priorities, and clinical standards set by executive leadership*

(JCAHO) and the **Centers for Medicare & Medicaid Services (CMS)** require hospitals to report quality measures, such as the percentage of eligible patients with acute myocardial infarction that are prescribed aspirin and beta blockers at hospital admission and discharge, and the percentage of patients admitted to the hospital with congestive heart failure who have a documented assessment of their left ventricular ejection fraction.[4] The **Agency for Healthcare Research and Quality (AHRQ)** maintains a clearinghouse of evidence-based quality measures,[5] and the **National Quality Forum (NQF)** endorses quality measures.[6]

Improving performance on these measures is an excellent target for CDS interventions, especially in circumstances when such improvement has a directly measurable return on investment (e.g., through a pay-for-performance initiative). An important step in determining objectives for a CDS program is, therefore, a careful assessment of external and internal quality initiatives that are affecting your organization, or might be soon.

CDS Functional Requirements and HIT Product Certification

Efforts are emerging to define necessary CDS functionality in CIS. Your organization may already be tracking them. These efforts include **healthcare information technology (HIT)** product certification by the **Certification Commission for Health Information Technology (CCHIT)**,[7] the **Leapfrog** CPOE testing protocol,[8] and minimum CDS requirements for electronic prescribing systems covered by the Medicare Modernization Act.[9] More broadly, the **Office of the National Coordinator for Health Information Technology (ONCHIT)**[10] in the United States is charged with facilitating "the effective use of information technology to improve the quality, efficiency, and safety of health care for all Americans." This office likely will play an increasing role in matters related to CDS deployment. All these evolving initiatives are currently in early stages; readers are encouraged to check their latest status to determine what, if any, specific implications these efforts might have for your CDS program.

Internal Drivers

Those who are or will become CDS stakeholders in your organization may have already identified key

---

* As with Figure 1, this is an iterative process.

CDS-related priorities, such as improving the safety or cost-effectiveness of patient care, before a formal CDS program begins. There might even be initiatives under way in specific areas to address these high-level goals, such as improving performance on individual **National Committee for Quality Assurance (NCQA) HEDIS** measures[11] or CMS hospital quality measures,[12] or addressing specific JCAHO[13] and NCQA[14] accreditation requirements.

The CDS program is a toolkit for addressing those goals. It will require resources to develop, deploy, and evaluate the knowledge delivery interventions. The management buy-in for addressing the goals and objectives can help with securing these resources. For example, if there is organizational commitment to a disease management initiative, this support can be leveraged to obtain software, CDS content, and staff time needed to implement CDS interventions that further enhance the initiative's effectiveness.

In addition, support from clinicians who are concerned about specific clinical goals can help drive the behavior change that will be required to deploy CDS interventions aimed at that goal. For example, modified workflows will often be required to incorporate the interventions into daily routines. This change may initially require effort and patience. The more those affected (and their management) understand how the interventions serve important

organizational and patient care needs, the more successful they are likely to be in making the necessary changes.

The success of both individual CDS interventions and the overall CDS program therefore depends heavily on the extent to which the organization and its leadership are involved. Numerous studies show that more than just well-designed and user-friendly CDS **applications** are needed. Intervention acceptance and success also depends on skillful attention to communication, implementation management, ongoing focus on overall goals, and strong commitment from leadership.[15] Figures 1-1 through 1-3 help identify the specific stakeholders in these activities and map their interactions within the CDS program. Organizations that have effectively deployed CDS interventions share success factors summarized in Figure 1-4.

Figure 1-5 lists some high-level goals that many healthcare organizations are working on and that could be addressed within a CDS program. These can serve as a starting point in thinking about what goals might be particularly opportune for CDS in your institution. Note that each CDS goal in this figure is broken down into more specific goals and objectives. This goal decomposition is a key step toward identifying appropriate CDS interventions, and will be explored in more detail shortly.

Figure 1-4: CDS program success factors

- Deep executive support for clinical quality improvement and belief in the value of information technology to help achieve it.

- A history of successful clinical information technology projects, fostering a strong belief among clinicians and organizational leaders that CIS are valuable and desirable tools.

- Excellent communication about the clinical and technological nature of the CDS program to all involved stakeholders.

- Involvement of key **users** and clinical champions well in advance of the implementation of any new CDS program.

- Strong support and rapid problem resolution by project staff before, and especially during, early implementation.

Figure 1-5: Examples of organizational CDS goals and corresponding clinical goals and objectives

High-level CDS Goal	Typical Clinical Goal	Typical Clinical Objective
Develop disease management/condition-specific initiatives to improve outcomes for particular complaints, diagnoses or procedures (e.g., diabetes)[16]	• Decrease complications associated with target diagnoses (e.g. diabetic kidney disease)	• Increase number of diabetics who receive annual screening for proteinuria
Improve overall care safety	• Minimize adverse drug events • Optimize critical information transfer among clinicians within hospitals, inpatient and outpatient clinicians, generalist and specialist clinicians	• Decrease occurrence of severe drug interactions • Decrease inadequate follow-up of critical test results, such as abnormal biopsies, radiological studies, and laboratory tests
Optimize reimbursement for care	• Increase percent of patients with target conditions who meet pay-for-performance criteria • Improve billing levels and appropriateness	• Increase percent of eligible patients with heart attack given beta blockers on arrival at the hospital • Improve coding levels from ambulatory encounters
Optimize cost-effectiveness of care	• Improve appropriateness of referrals • Reduce unnecessary tests • Reduce inpatient length of stay	• Reduce unnecessary referrals for Pap smears • Reduce overly-frequent x-ray studies
Enhance patient education and empowerment	• Optimize patient adherence with indicated screening tests for preventive care	• Increase percentage of eligible women who receive screening mammography
Foster compliance with clinical guidelines,[17] evidence-based practice,[18] and reporting and regulatory requirements[19]	• Optimize performance on specific quality measures	• Offer Chlamydia screening to all eligible women
Address clinicians' recognized and unrecognized information needs	• Provide "just-in-time" relevant treatment information for a disease/condition, within clinical workflow	• Address the majority of questions clinicians pose to computer-based resources within two minutes

Determining CDS Targets

The discussion about identifying stakeholders and categorizing potential CDS goals outlined above provides the framework for determining high-priority targets that your organization will address with CDS interventions. A variety of processes that can help with this selection, some of which your organization already may be using, are outlined in Figure 1-6.

It is often the case, especially in larger organizations, that there are relatively independent efforts focused on similar objectives. For example, two different clinical departments might be pursuing care improvement efforts (such as focusing on safer and more effective heparin administration) that could benefit from richer cross-fertilization. Identifying such synergies is an important benefit of a thorough environmental analysis for the CDS program.

The survey of local initiatives may uncover potential new goals and objectives. For example, discussions with key stakeholders might reveal that some of the issues listed in Figure 1-5 are not being addressed but should be. As you flesh out the specific targets of greatest importance to address in the CDS program, you can consider some of the categories and examples outlined in Figure 1-7.

Ideal targets for CDS interventions might be

- Patient management issues that occur frequently;
- Activities that are associated with a significant gap in performance or a missed opportunity to optimize care;
- Care events in which the performance shortfall substantially boosts clinical costs or lowers quality and safety; and
- Activities in which performance can be improved through better distribution of knowledge, improved communication or heightened awareness.

Issues that occur less frequently, but which could have catastrophic consequences, are also potentially attractive candidates for decision support interventions. Figure 1-8, page 10, is a draft heuristic that illustrates how these factors relate in suggesting the overall desirability of addressing any individual objective.

Once an organization begins deploying CDS interventions, various stakeholders typically approach those responsible for the CDS program with requests to add new interventions that address specific needs. Standards for how such requests are submitted and prioritized can be helpful in ensur-

---

Figure 1-6: Sources for determining CDS targets

- Institutional analyses of quality, safety, patient satisfaction, cost, and regulatory problems (e.g., from committees such as pharmacy and therapeutics, quality assurance, patient safety, utilization review, or others)

- High-level committees that prepare the overall response to environmental drivers, such as accreditation requirements (e.g., related to care safety and quality), pay-for-performance, and related quality measurement/improvement initiatives

- Technology-supported analyses and mining of local care and outcomes, conducted in-house[20] or with support from vendors

- Interviews with clinicians, medical directors, and other stakeholders

- Surveys assessing stakeholders' CDS-related activities, needs, and priorities

- Direct observation of information needs in clinical settings

- Community-based priorities and programs

Figure 1-7: Some categories and examples of clinical goals and objectives

Target	Examples/References
• **Clinical interventions** for which there is strong evidence that patient benefit outweighs potential harm	• Interventions identified in evidence-based **clinical practice guidelines**[21] • Interventions marked as "beneficial" in Clinical Evidence[22] • Findings in AHRQ Evidence Reports[23]
• Clinical interventions for which trials have demonstrated that CDS approaches are or might be effective in improving healthcare processes and outcomes[24]	• Practices supported by evidence[25] • Practitioner performance[26] • Medication safety[27] • Disease management[28] • Chronic care management[29]
• Institute of Medicine (IOM) priority areas for transforming healthcare quality	• Asthma, diabetes, hypertension, immunizations, patient self-management[16]
• National quality measures, especially those being investigated in "pay for performance" pilots (such as those linked to management of acute myocardial infarction, community acquired pneumonia, heart failure, among others)	• CMS Hospital Quality Initiative[30] • Medicare Physician Group Practice Demonstration[31] • JCAHO/CMS initiative to align hospital performance measures[32] • Leapfrog Group; Rewarding Results[33] • Bridges to Excellence[34]
• Results of systematic analyses of clinical errors or quality problems	• USP MedMarx database[35] • HHS patient safety reporting systems[36] • McGlynn et al. The Quality of Health Care Delivered to Adults in the United States[37] • NCQA State of Health Care Quality report[38] • Preventing adverse drug events[39] • Types of medical errors[40]
• CDS interventions addressed in CIS certification programs, and government-supported CIS initiatives	• Certification Commission for Health Information Technology[7] • e-prescribing covered under Medicare Modernization Act[9] • Doctors' Office Quality Information Technology (DOQ-IT)[41]

Figure 1-8: Factors affecting the desirability of a CDS objective

Clinical Objective Value Score = (P+O+C+N+G)-(D+C), where*

P= Patient impact (individual/population) (positive, e.g., quality, safe, cost-effective care; improved morbidity and mortality, of interest to patients)

O= Organizational impact (positive, e.g., regulatory or audit compliance, appropriate resource use, liability)

C= Clinician impact (favorable, e.g. enhanced workflow; consistent with consensus, local standards, feasible to address, of interest to clinicians)

N= Number of patients positively affected

G= Gap between ideal and actual behavior pertinent to the intervention

D= Difficulty associated with addressing the objective

C= Cost of addressing the objective

---

ing that limited resources for implementing CDS interventions are effectively applied. The variables and relationships in Figure 1-8 can be used in this prioritization.

Keep in mind that just because an organization has the capability to deliver CDS interventions, this might not necessarily be the most appropriate response for every problem. In some cases, a better approach might involve some care process modification (to workflow or policies) that does not involve clinical knowledge delivery.

Stakeholders Revisited
Identifying Champions

Dialogue about potential CDS goals, objectives, and strategies will primarily involve the governance and management levels in Figure 1-2. As these interactions unfold, various stakeholders might take a range of positions regarding the CDS targets and the prospect of addressing them with CDS interventions. Those who are strongly supportive of the CDS program in general, or specific interventions, are potential champions.

Identifying and cultivating champions early in the process is an important component of success.

Champions represent the interests of the front-line users and form a vital bridge between the proponents of a CDS program or intervention, and the front-line clinicians, staff, patients, and others whose activities will be most affected by CDS. Champions have been defined as "the smallest group of persons to whom everyone else will listen." They should have considerable involvement early in the development of a program or intervention; their concerns should be heard and addressed attentively. In turn, champions can help explain the emerging CDS program to their peers, speaking as a trusted colleague, and win and maintain support at the executive and management levels.

In addition to looking for champions among formal governance and management leadership, consider other opinion leaders in the organization to whom others will listen. This latter group can exert substantial influence over the collective attitude of an organization toward the CDS strategies and tactics. These people may include leading clinicians, others who may have achieved recognition for their work, and prominent patient advocates.

---

* The strength of objective, systematic evidence about the magnitude of the variable should be considered when practical.

Working with Implementation Champions

Many of the tasks outlined below will occur during the implementation phases of the CDS program described in later chapters. However, understanding the full scope of potential work with champions early in the process can help you establish a solid and extensible foundation for collaborating with these stakeholders throughout the program life cycle.

In later implementation stages, such as CDS intervention development, testing, and **rollout,** a broad set of stakeholders will come into play. These include departments and roles where work relates to the clinical objectives of interest, or might be affected by corresponding CDS interventions. Also involved are those who capture data necessary to trigger clinical **alerts, reminders,** and other proactive CDS interventions. Champions should be sought among these groups to ensure that all available support is effectively utilized from those who will be affected by the program. Note that this broader set of implementation stakeholders can come from all levels in Figure 1-2.

After identifying who might serve as a champion for one or more CDS interventions, the next step is to engage these individuals to support the program. Asking departmental and administration leaders for nominations can effectively leverage the organizational structure, but other volunteers also should be widely and directly solicited. Demonstrations of the proposed interventions may help enlist this support. In addition, direct observation of individuals performing their jobs both may help identify those whose jobs may be affected by the interventions as well as provide a natural opportunity to recruit such individuals as champions.

A process should be put in place for developing and maintaining champions as a productive and helpful resource for the CDS program. Training on the technical and clinical aspects of proposed interventions is important so that all champions share a common and accurate understanding of the use, advantages, and limitations of the proposed system. Regularly requesting advice from the champions about system issues (configuration, interface design, content of interventions, etc.) and deployment issues, and then providing feedback regarding the disposition of these suggestions, is important to give the champions a sense of project ownership and to maintain their motivation.

In turn, the champions can serve as ambassadors to their co-workers and departments in promoting the interventions, supporting training efforts, soliciting advice, providing feedback, and helping in other ways as an ongoing resource for promoting successful intervention use and evolution. For CDS interventions likely to be controversial and/or disruptive to workflow, working closely with champions as a link to the affected community can mean the difference between intervention success and failure.

Since the time commitment required of champions can be significant and their role can be so essential to CDS program success, many organizations will compensate key champions. This often takes the form of including this role explicitly in job responsibilities and setting aside work time specifically to accomplish pertinent tasks. However, not all champions require compensation, especially for more modest levels of program support. For many, the opportunity to help shape the CDS program and generate its **desired outcomes** may be ample compensation.

Not Everyone Is a Champion

Many stakeholders will not be as positive about the CDS program and interventions as the champions. Thoughtful individuals might be neutral, or be "**resistors**" who push back, or "**detractors**" who actively work against the proposed plan. Keep in mind that these individuals may be those whose work is affected in some way by the intervention, as well as those who are its intended recipients. It is essential to engage resistors and detractors in active dialogue—they can be a critical source of feedback about the program and play an important role in its success or failure.

The CDS team should work to fully understand their concerns, since usually they reflect legitimate issues with the underlying approach. As such, these concerns should be addressed to the extent practical, particularly for any common themes that emerge. This should be done early in the development and implementation process to reduce problems later that could potentially derail the intervention or program.

Solid clinical leadership can help minimize the negative effects from issues that cannot immediately be resolved. This leadership involves clearly setting goals and expectations, communicating often and effectively, and modeling and reinforcing desired behaviors regarding the CDS program. Implementers often find that thoughtful attention to resistors' and detractors' concerns will convert them into the most fervent champions. We will revisit working with champions, resistors, and detractors in subsequent chapters.

Cost-justifying the CDS Program and Preparing to Realize Benefits

Selecting, developing or procuring, deploying, and evaluating CDS interventions to improve outcomes will consume a significant amount of your organization's limited resources, including time, attention, effort, staff and capital. Reaping the desired clinical and financial return on this investment requires careful attention and effort focused on benefits realization.

Benefits Planning and Realization

Benefits realization from clinical information systems requires a systematic approach. Experts in this field are beginning to define its essential elements.[42] Key organizational steps to realizing benefits from clinical information systems (including CDS interventions) are listed below, with each followed by the chapter in this book that explores that step in depth.

- Organizing for benefits with a benefits realization team (Chapter 1);

- Designing explicitly for benefits (Chapter 3);
- Planning for benefits by addressing change management issues during system implementation (Chapters 4 and 5);
- Measuring the benefits (Chapter 6); and
- Accountability for benefits (Chapter 6).

So far in this chapter we have discussed examining organizational structures *already in place* that might interplay with CDS interventions individually or with a more comprehensive CDS program. More robust CDS programs will generally require new, or at least modified, organizational roles and teams. One such team to consider is a performance improvement or benefits realization team.

The CDS goals and clinical goals and objectives outlined in Figure 1-5 are associated with the business goals listed in Figure 1-9. A benefits realization team can assume responsibility for defining and validating these goals and objectives, helping determine accountability for the benefits, ensuring that CDS interventions and corresponding process changes help achieve them, and measuring and reporting progress toward the targets. This team can also help educate internal stakeholders about the expected benefits and efforts to realize them, and report the achieved benefits externally if desired (e.g., via journal articles or society meetings).

In smaller organizations or narrowly focused CDS programs, available resources might be limited to a single individual and role responsible for these functions. Conversely, in large organizations or comprehensive programs, the functions might be spread across several roles and groups outlined in Figure 1-2.

To accomplish these goals, a benefits realization team ideally includes individuals with technical expertise; clinical, administrative and financial operational experience; and medical informatics-related health services research experience. Because CDS interventions often involve many areas in the organization, the benefits realization team should be richly interdepartmental. However, it should be more than a collection of department heads or rep-

Figure 1-9: Types of business benefits that can accrue from CDS programs

- Reduced resource wasted due to redundant and inefficient activities to support clinicians' decision making
- Reduced costs of care (e.g., via more appropriate testing, cheaper and more appropriately utilized medications and therapies, reduced staff rework and better care delivery coordination)
- Reduced costs associated with medical errors (e.g., from legal liability and averted safety problems, and additional work, tests, therapies to remediate them)
- Reduced liability insurance premiums based on demonstrably improved safety
- Increased revenue (e.g., from pay for performance incentives)
- Increased market share (e.g., from more engaged and satisfied patients and demonstration of high-quality process and outcomes)
- Improved staff retention (e.g., by providing a high quality professional knowledge management and decision support environment)
- Improved staff utilization (e.g., redeploy QA nurse from chart reviews to CDS implementation)
- Enhanced leverage to improve outcomes from investments (and data) in CIS
- Enhanced quality of healthcare professional education provided by the organization
- Improved health services research capabilities and ability to attract grants

resentatives. Creating a benefits realization *function* to underpin the team enables focus beyond the sum of individual operating department responsibilities. This combination of expertise and participation will help ensure that new CDS interventions are effective and that analyses of these effects are credible. Because the CDS targets are generally closely related to the organization's core mission, the CDS benefits team should report directly or indirectly to executive leadership.

Cost Justification

It is against this backdrop of anticipated benefits that the costs associated with CDS interventions and programs should be approached. For some organizations, this investment is implicitly considered necessary to accomplish its clinical quality-related mission. In other organizations, a more explicit justification will be helpful to obtain the needed resources and

support. If initial CDS interventions (e.g., links to online reference materials) will be implemented for some reason in a very limited way without involving organizational governance, then cost-justification at this point might not be a major issue.

Many organizations using this book will already have made substantial investments in CIS, perhaps including CPOE or EMR, and will, therefore, have a framework for cost-justifying the CDS program elements. Though there might be a tendency to consider this program as a component of the IT strategy (especially if its resources are budgeted under IT), its broader implications and more direct coupling with the organization's overall strategy should be clear by now.

As with any cost-justification, it is important to compare the full spectrum of resources consumed and benefits realized both with and without the new approach that is the subject of the cost-justification; in this case, an individual CDS intervention or a suite of such interventions within a CDS program. The cost justification, therefore, includes considering resources such as staff, dollars, time, and energy currently applied in addressing a particular goal or objective. It also includes the results achieved from this investment, with the costs and results associated with a more coordinated approach to applying knowledge resources to address the target.

Consider, for example, the case of medication safety. In many organizations there are a variety of stakeholders in addressing these needs (e.g., patients, nursing, pharmacy, medical staff, and pharmacy and therapeutics committee) who might not be working on this important issue in an optimally effective and efficient manner. Besides the direct costs (e.g., related to adverse drug events) and quality implications of a suboptimal organizational approach to medication management, the time spent by pharmacy and therapeutics committees and other stakeholders on these matters can be very expensive. Cost savings can be realized through a more focused and coordinated approach to delivering essential knowledge to stakeholders (e.g., via well deployed reference information, alerts, and calls by pharmacists) that would emerge by addressing this issue within a carefully developed CDS program. These savings can accrue as a result of targeting resources to high-yield opportunities for improvement, reducing redundant and inefficient efforts, and avoiding quality and safety problems (and their associated costs) that might otherwise slip through a fragmented safety net.[43]

In general, cost-justifications and performance improvement targets should be based on available literature when possible. A variety of studies have suggested that substantial savings can accrue from applying CDS to the medication management process. For example, preventable adverse drug events in hospitals have been estimated to generate $4,685 in excess costs per event, averaging $2.8 million for a 700-bed teaching hospital.[44] An analysis of CPOE in ambulatory settings suggests that $2 billion could be saved in the U.S. through

their ability to prevent these adverse events.[45] One hospital described a $5–10 million return on investment from its advanced CDS interventions.[46] Other analyses have yielded lower estimates for the cost of adverse drug events, but even if the actual savings are only a fraction of the higher estimates, the financial benefits to an organization over time would be quite substantial. This is especially true when one factors in costs associated with litigating and settling malpractice actions resulting from adverse drug events, and the suboptimal use of staff time in preventing these events.

The business benefits outlined in Figure 1-9 that can accrue from well-implemented CDS programs can be used to generate financial benefits estimates needed for cost justification. The first bullet in the figure speaks to inefficiencies and other problems associated with procuring, maintaining and disseminating knowledge interventions on mission-critical matters in a suboptimal and uncoordinated manner across an organization. This item alone leads some organizations to ask, "How many versions of the truth can we afford to support?" and conclude that they cannot afford *not* to have a coordinated CDS program to address high-priority goals.

Analyzing the anticipated costs and benefits of a proposed CDS program in the context of current practices provides the foundation for a business case for the program, including areas likely to produce the greatest yield. While it will be straightforward to quantify some elements, other elements (e.g., healthier and more satisfied patients) may not be directly quantifiable, though their intangible or strategic value should be documented nonetheless. If a benefits realization team is in place or can be adapted from other existing teams, it would naturally serve as the focal point for developing this case. In many instances, though, the impetus for creating a CDS benefits realization or performance improvement team will arise as a response to an initial business case (formal or informal) for the CDS program.

Business literature and other resources are available to help those organizations interested in formal cost justification.[47] In these cases, it is useful to work closely with the organization's financial officer on articulating the CDS program's clinical, strategic and financial value, in addition to the costs.

Chapter 6 will discuss in detail assessing the value of the CDS program after it has been implemented. At that point you will validate the value proposition you began establishing at the program's inception.

WORKSHEETS

This book is intended to support the development of a comprehensive organizational approach to improving outcomes with CDS; it is also intended to support the development of individual interventions surrounding a single goal or objective. For many institutions, it is assumed that the organizational survey of stakeholders and goals will be comprehensive. The resulting CDS program, therefore, will ultimately be broad in scope and deep in interventions deployed to address the wide range of clinical goals. In other organizations, a CDS program will begin as a more focused effort to address a particular need with a focused group of stakeholders.

In either case, CDS interventions will focus on specific goals. Since many of the worksheets focus on managing individual goals, there will actually be a set of worksheets that characterizes the activity pertinent to each separate goal within the CDS program. For example, two sample versions are presented below for Worksheet 1-1. The first addresses the stakeholders and goals pertinent to a comprehensive CDS program, and the second is directed toward a more focused CDS initiative. Depending on the scope of your CDS initiative, you can either attempt to consolidate all elements of your CDS program pertinent to each worksheet in one document or maintain a set of worksheets corresponding to the various goals covered by your program.

Step 1: Identify and contact the key local committees, positions, and individuals currently in place that will have a stake in the CDS program, either by proposing, validating, sup-

A Note on the Worksheets and CDS Program Scope

The worksheets are designed so that you can actually use them to gather and analyze data in the process of building your CDS program. Throughout this book, we have included recommendations and sample data to give you an idea of how to fill in each worksheet. The CDS goal of improving anticoagulation management, together with related CDS interventions, threads throughout the sample worksheets to illustrate how the data builds and the program unfolds from sheet to sheet. Blank, electronic versions of worksheets are available from the book's Web site (www.himss.org/cdsguide) for you to download and use.

We recommend compiling these worksheets into a notebook. This is a convenient way to bring together documentation on all the details of your unfolding CDS program (e.g., its specific goals and objectives, CDS interventions, and results). The notebook (in print and/or an electronic version) can be a useful tool in the many different interactions with stakeholders recommended throughout this book. These include developing and getting feedback on CDS targets, creating and validating intervention specifications, and evaluating results and planning enhancements. It also provides a detailed, tangible source for answers to questions about the history, status, and plans for the CDS program.

porting, communicating, or using the CDS interventions (see Figure 1-1, page 3). Begin considering their current roles and activities and how they might relate to a more coordinated CDS program. Consider also new positions and teams that might be needed to ensure the program's success. Use Worksheet 1-1 to document potential CDS goals and clinical goals and objectives of importance to, or already being addressed at, your organization.

You can use Figure 1-1 to create a list of key stakeholders in your organization's current and emerging CDS efforts and begin assessing their current and potential role in these efforts. Think broadly about potential stakeholders, as suggested in the stakeholder discussion on pages 17–18. For example, pay careful attention to those individuals whose behavior might require change due to the CDS program.

In your survey, broadly consider the scope of potential CDS initiatives (e.g., as suggested by Figures 1-5 and 1-7) to avoid missing important opportunities that might otherwise be overlooked. Look carefully at the case management activities in your organization. These initiatives often are quite labor-intensive and could be ripe for CDS interventions. If your organization has or is contemplating a clinical transformation process to improve operations and outcomes, seek ways to ensure that this transformation process and the CDS program are mutually supportive and tightly integrated.

Similarly, look for pertinent initiatives under the following headings: patient safety, quality improvement, care improvement, clinical pathways, disease management, or strategic initiatives. These, too, will be prime candidates for tight integration with the organization's CDS efforts.

Specific CDS goals and objectives that are important in your organization will emerge from dialogue with the stakeholders listed in Figure 1-1. Worksheet 1-1 can be used to document these discussions. CDS interventions focused on issues of

greatest importance to the organization will have the best opportunity to succeed.

Because different constituencies (such as management, clinicians, and patients) might have different perspectives on the importance of each goal or objective, consider these perspectives individually and collectively. For example, CDS interventions focused on goals that are a high priority for management, clinicians, and patients will likely receive the sustained focus and support that are required for successful implementation. Conversely, interventions focused on goals that are of low priority to one or more of these constituents will have less chance of succeeding.

Strong imbalances in the priority given to a goal or objective among different stakeholders can indicate the need for dialogue and education to achieve a shared vision on the issue. Reconciling such differences before specific CDS interventions focused on the goal are developed and implemented could save significant time, aggravation, and money.

Step 2: Synthesize and validate a working list of CDS goals, and clinical goals and objectives for your CDS program. Define baseline and target performance for the clinical objectives.

The analysis in Worksheet 1-1 of current and potential clinical goals within your organization provides the foundation for synthesizing and prioritizing the CDS program goals. Prioritizing can be important if limited resources or other factors tightly constrain the number of issues that the CDS program can contemplate at one time. It might be useful to first begin developing detailed clinical goals and objectives for the CDS goals and focus areas that are expected, based on Worksheet 1-1 data, to be of greatest importance to your organization.

In Worksheet 1-1 you began breaking down clinical goals into measurable objectives based on stakeholder discussions. It is important to think more comprehensively about the range of objectives that might be helpful in achieving the goal. To help prepare for measuring progress toward CDS targets, Worksheet 1-2 includes a column for documenting

Worksheet 1-1:
Stakeholders, goals, and objectives

*This worksheet is used to document your discussions with stakeholders about their priority clinical goals and objectives, as outlined in this chapter. Careful attention to **all** key stakeholders cannot be overemphasized. With Figures 1-1 and 1-2 as guides, list each stakeholder in the first column.*

In the next column, indicate the role that this person or group will play in the CDS program (e.g., from Figure 1-2). You should also note whether they are a potential champion or resistor/detractor for addressing a particular goal or objective (that you will list in the next columns) with CDS interventions, and whether they might play a key role in obtaining resources or funding.

In the third column, list the high level clinical goals that emerged from your discussions as important to this person or committee. These goals define broad care processes or outcomes that you will address with CDS interventions. Besides listening for spontaneously-offered stakeholder priorities, use the sources in Figure 1-6 to probe for organizational focus on the goals in Figure 1-5.

In the fourth column, break down the goals you have elicited into their component clinical objectives. The more specific and quantifiable you make these objectives, the more likely you will be to devise interventions that produce measurable results. For example, an objective such as "improve prescribing practices for heparin" will likely be less useful than a more specific one, such as "decrease incidence of heparin overdose."

Example 1: Focused Program

Stakeholder(s) (Title)	Role	High Level Clinical Goals	Clinical Objectives
Melinda B. (Chief Medical Officer)	Proponent, clinical thought leader; budget owner	Anticoagulant safety	Improve subcutaneous heparin prophylaxis for post-surgical patients
John A. (Chief Nursing Officer)	Proponent, clinical thought leader	Anticoagulant safety	• Reduce bleeding complications in the cardiology areas • Improve checking of partial thromboplastin time (PTT) in patients on intravenous (IV) heparin • Improve checking of CBC in patients on IV heparin • Improve compliance with care guideline for when to choose subcutaneous heparin versus low molecular weight heparin

Worksheet 1-1 *continued*

Example 2: Comprehensive Program

Stakeholder(s)	Role in CDS Program	High Level Goals	Clinical Objectives
James C. (Chief Quality Officer)	Proponent, general quality leader	Disease-specific prevention (outpatient)	• Improve checking of urinary protein and eye exams in diabetics • Improve prescription patterns for asthmatics on inhaled steroids
		Antibiotic utilization (inpatient)	Improve compliance with antibiotic prescriptions based on culture data
Claire D. (Chief Nursing Officer)	Detractor	Accuracy of nursing documentation	Improve likelihood of advanced directives being reviewed with patients
			Improve accuracy of allergy documentation
Ken V. (Director of ICU)	Proponent, clinical thought leader	Ventilator management	Reduce number of patients receiving paralytics
			Reduce ventilator-associated lung injuries
		Management of pressors for blood pressure support	Reduce use of high dose norepinephrine as opposed to multiple pressors
Eric E. (Director of Oncology Service)	Proponent, clinical thought leader	Management of patients in bone marrow unit	Decrease likelihood of high dose chemotherapy being started too late after admission
			Reduce vancomycin over-utilization in patients with neutropenic fever

Worksheet 1-2:
Objectives and performance

This worksheet helps integrate, prioritize, and refine the survey of clinical goals and objectives. You can generate a separate version for each of the priority high-level clinical goals you documented in Worksheet 1-1; these goals are listed at the top of each copy of Worksheet 1-2. Much of the data needed to complete this worksheet will be derived from interactions with stakeholders and committees as part of completing Worksheet 1-1. Therefore, you can begin working on Worksheet(s) 1-2 as part of that survey as soon as key themes begin to emerge.

In the first column of each version of Worksheet 1-2, you can more comprehensively define a set of clinical objectives required to achieve the goal. Then, in the second column, you can identify workflow-based processes and actions that will address each objective. For each action, use the third column to document (as quantitatively as is practical) the baseline performance level of that action. The fourth column is used to record the desired outcomes (again, ideally in a quantifiable way) that would indicate success in achieving the objective.

Several key issues mentioned above should be recorded in the Notes column. These include rationale for pursuing the objective, key stakeholder(s), and major initiatives currently in place to address this objective. In addition, matters pertinent to CDS cost-justification (e.g., inefficiencies and opportunities in current approaches) should be documented as well.

Your stakeholder and environmental survey of CDS opportunities may identify more important clinical goals than can comfortably be addressed at this stage of your program. The information in the notes column can help prioritize your Worksheet(s) 1-2 (i.e., those with the strongest momentum, rationale, cost/benefit opportunity) and might be logical choices for next-round CDS efforts.

The example below uses the focused example from Worksheet 1-1.

Clinical goal: Anticoagulation Improvement Program

Clinical Objective	Desired Action	Baseline Performance	Desired Outcomes	Notes
Improve post-op heparin prophylaxis	Entry of physician order for subcutaneous heparin	Review of inpatient order entry data reveals approximately 62% compliance on the three surgical wards.	100% compliance for appropriate patients, defined as no history of neurosurgery or other major bleeding risk and no history of heparin related allergy or problem in the past	Objective is big push for quality officer; lots of time and attention being devoted to the gap; interest in exploring CDS to help make current improvement approach more efficient and effective
Improve monitoring for PTT on a timely and regular basis	Order for PTT entered by physician	88% of reviewed patients have PTT ordered within the first six hours	100% compliance	

Worksheet 1-2 *continued*

Clinical Objective	Desired Action	Baseline Performance	Desired Outcomes	Notes
	Collection of PTT by nursing	66% of reviewed patients had PTT collected within the first six hours	100% compliance	Some wards are not staffed with nursing assistants, leading to delays in drawing the PTT
	Reporting of PTT by clinical laboratory	59% of reviewed patients had PTT reported within the first six hours	90% compliance, allow for some delay based on time of day and lab reporting schedule, but only one hour leeway	Shift changes seem to have a big effect on the delay to reporting of PTT
Improve compliance with care guideline for enoxaparin and subcutaneous heparin	Order for enoxaparin in patients admitted with deep vein thrombosis without embolism	75% of hospitalized patients with DVT still receive IV heparin	100% compliance with enoxaparin and DVT policy	

measurable **baseline performance** levels and desired outcomes.

Worksheet 1-2 is a sample CDS program goal worksheet that illustrates the process of articulating **clinical objectives** and desired actions necessary to accomplish specific high-level clinical goals. You will likely complete this set of worksheets for your CDS program over time, building, refining, prioritizing, and validating their contents during multiple meetings with internal stakeholders and based on other research as discussed above.

An explicit and detailed picture of care improvement opportunities emerges from completed Worksheet(s) 1-2. They should trigger a thoughtful gap analysis, i.e., an effort to understand the care structure and processes that result in the difference between the current and desired performance.

This analysis is an essential prerequisite to developing successful improvement strategies that will help uncover promising modifications to informa-

tion management and workflow. These strategies may include CDS interventions, but do not assume that this will always be the case. Despite the focus of this book on these knowledge-based interventions, it is important to recognize that these might not always be the best or first approach to addressing every performance gap; the analysis will help identify their proper role.

CONCLUDING COMMENTS

The extent to which careful attention to stakeholder needs and related organizational processes can help ensure a CDS program's success cannot be overstated. Time invested early in the process to fully understand the needs and motivations of all stakeholders in the program will provide a payback in later implementation stages. Likewise, capitalizing on existing organizational momentum toward what will become CDS program goals and objectives can help overcome the obstacles that the program inevitably will encounter and ensure its ultimate success.

After completing this section, you will have working documents (Worksheets 1-2) that define your CDS program targets in detail. These documents can help provide a clear and shared vision of these targets for all the stakeholders in Figure 1-2. Although substantial effort is required to get to this point, the list should remain dynamic. Expect that as the CDS implementation process unfolds, the targets and priorities will evolve, perhaps as a result of new insights, or changes within the local environment and in the external forces in healthcare acting upon it.

The implications of addressing the issues discussed in this section go beyond the CDS program itself. For example, the detailed articulation of goals and objectives for clinical improvement in Worksheet 1-2 could be the most complete synthesis of these issues in your organization. As such, they could be useful for addressing the targets in ways other than the primarily computer-based approaches discussed in this book. For example, they might suggest workflow reorganization and other mechanisms to help achieve the goals.

The next chapter will help you assess your information systems infrastructure that is available for selecting specific interventions (discussed in Chapter 3) that will be used to accomplish the program's goals and objectives.

References

1 See, for example, Kotter JP, Cohen DS. *The Heart of Change: Real-Life Stories of How People Change Their Organizations.* Cambridge, MA: Harvard Business School Publishing; 2002.

2 Kaplan R, Norton D. Using the balanced scorecard as a strategic management system. *Harv Bus Rev.* 1996;74(1):75–85.

3 The Leapfrog Group maintains a Web-based compendium of incentive and reward programs aimed at improving care that provides details on scores of these programs (http://www.leapfroggroup.org/leapfrog_compendium).

4 Both JCAHO and CMS require reporting of "core measures." They are working toward convergence of these requirements; details can be found at http://www.jcaho.org/pms/core+measures/aligned_manual.htm and http://www.cms.hhs.gov/quality/hospital.

5 http://www.qualitymeasures.ahrq.gov.

6 http://www.qualityforum.org.

7 http://www.cchit.org.

8 http://www.leapfroggroup.org/media/file/Leapfrog-Computer_Physician_Order_Entry_Fact_Sheet.pdf.

9 Teich JM, Osheroff JA, et al. *Clinical Decision Support in Electronic Prescribing: Recommendations and an Action Plan.* Report for the Department of HHS. March 2005. *J Am Med Informatics Assoc* 12(4), July/Aug 2005 (in press). Also available at http://www.amia.org/pubs/whitepapers/docs/cdswhitepaperforhhs-final2005-03-08.pdf.

10 http://www.hhs.gov/healthit.

11 National Committee for Quality Assurance. What is HEDIS? http://www.ncqa.org/Programs/HEDIS.

12 http://www.cms.hhs.gov/quality/hospital.

13 Joint Commission on Accreditation of Healthcare Organizations. Position statement on reporting medical errors. http://www.jcaho.org/accredited+organizations/patient+safety/medical+errors+disclosure/index.htm.

14 National Committee for Quality Assurance. Accreditation parameters. http://www.ncqa.org/Programs/Accreditation/MCO/mcostdsoverview.htm. Note especially quality improvement processes.

15 See, for example, manuscripts of organizations that have won the Davies Award for Excellence in EHR Implementation: http://www.himss.org/asp/davies_organizational.asp.

16 For a list of topics identified nationally as high priority for this type of program see the following: Institute of Medicine (IOM). *Priority Areas for National Action: Transforming Health Care Quality.* 2003. (A summary is available at http://www.ahrq.gov/qual/iompriorities.htm; the full report is available at http://www.nap.edu/books/0309085438/html); see the AHRQ priority topics for research at http://www.ahrq.gov/about/mmarsrch.htm.

17 For example, note recent increased emphasis on implementing guidelines in practice (*Ann Intern Med.* 2003;139:6, 493–498). Consider guideline types as outlined in the 1992 IOM report and discussed in the 1998 *JAMIA* (http://www.jamia.org/cgi/content/abstract/5/4/357). The guideline types and examples provided by the Institute's report include screening and prevention (vaccination for pregnant women who are planning international travel); diagnosis and pre-diagnosis management of patients (evaluation of chest pain in the emergency department); indications for use of surgical procedures (indications for carotid endarterectomy); appropriate use of specific technologies and tests as part of clinical care (use of autologous or donor blood for transfusions); and

guidelines for care of clinical conditions (management of patients following coronary-artery bypass graft).

18 E.g., see Figure 1-7, row 1.

19 Such as JCAHO/NCQA accreditation and quality measures (e.g., NCQA/HEDIS) and those in the National Healthcare Quality Report (http://www.ahcpr.gov/qual/nhqr02/premeasures.htm), the National Quality Measures Clearinghouse (http://www.qualitymeasures.ahrq.gov/browse/browsecondition.aspx), and the National Quality Forum hospital performance measures (http://www.qualityforum.org/txhospmeasBEACHpublic.pdf).

20 E.g., as described in Evans RS, Gardner RM, Bush AR, et al. Development of a computerized infectious disease monitor (CIDM). *Comput Biomed Res.* 1985; Apr;18(2):103–13.

21 National Guideline Clearinghouse, http://www.guidelines.gov.

22 BMJ Publishing Group, Clinical Evidence Web site, http://www.clinicalevidence.com.

23 Agency for Healthcare Research and Quality. Evidence-Based Practice: http://www.ahrq.gov/clinic/epcix.htm.

24 Users' Guides to the Medical Literature: XVIII. How to use an article evaluating the clinical impact of a computer-based clinical decision support system. *JAMA.* http://www.ucl.ac.uk/kmc/publications/pdfs/JAMA1999.pdf.

25 Agency for Healthcare Research and Quality. Making health care safer: a critical analysis of patient safety practices. AHRQ, July 2001, http://www.ahrq.gov/clinic/ptsafety/summrpt.htm. See especially the 11 practices strongly supported by evidence, and Chapter 53, clinical decision support systems.

26 Garg AX, Adhikari NKJ, McDonald H, Rosas-Arellano MP, Devereaux PJ, Beyene J, et al. Effects of computerized clinical decision support systems on performance and patient outcomes: a systematic review. *JAMA.* 2005; 293:1223–1238.

27 Kaushal R, Shojania K, Bates D. Effects of computerized physician order entry and clinical decision support systems on medication safety: a systematic review. *Arch Intern Med.* 2003;163:1409–1416.

28 Weingarten SR, et al. Interventions used in disease management programs for patients with chronic illness: which ones work? Meta-analysis of published reports. *BMJ.* 2002;323:925.

29 Rundall TG, et al. As good as it gets? Chronic care management in nine leading U.S. physician organizations. *BMJ.* 2002:325:958–61.

30 See http://www.cms.hhs.gov/quality/hospital (scroll down the page to see the variety of quality measurement and improvement initiatives).

31 See http://www.cms.hhs.gov/researchers/demos/pgp.asp.

32 See http://www.jcaho.org/pms/core+measures/aligned_manual.htm.

33 Rewarding results: aligning incentives with high-quality healthcare. http://www.leapfroggroup.org/RewardingResults. See also footnotes to quality measures in footnote to Figure 1-1.

34 National Committee for Quality Assurance. *Bridges to Excellence: Rewarding Quality across the Healthcare System.* http://www.ncqa.org/Programs/bridgestoexcellence/.

35 U.S. Pharmacopeia, National Database for Medication Errors. https://www.medmarx.com. See also America's riskiest drugs. *Forbes.* February 24, 2003. http://www.forbes.com/2003/02/24/cx_mh_0224risk.html.

36 Agency for Healthcare Research Quality. Patient safety reporting systems. http://www.ahrq.gov/qual/taskforce/hhsrepor.htm.

37 McGlynn, et al. The quality of healthcare delivered to adults in the United States. *New Engl J Med.* 2003; 348:2635–2645.

38 National Committee for Quality Assurance. *The State of Health Care Quality.* 2004. www.ncqa.org/communications/SOMC/SOHC2004.pdf.

39 Gurwitz, et al. Incidence and preventability of adverse drug events among older persons in the ambulatory setting. *JAMA.* 2003;289:1107–16.

40 Dovey SM, Phillips RL, Green LA, Fryer GE. Types of medical errors commonly reported by family physicians. *Am Fam Physician.* 2003;67:697.

41 See http://www.doqit.org/doqit/jsp/index.jsp.

42 Thompson DI, Henry S, Lockwood L, Anderson B, Atkinson S. Benefits planning for advanced clinical information systems implementation at Allina Hospitals and Clinic. *JHIM.* 2005;19(1);54–62. The HIMSS CIS Benefits Task Force is building a database of CIS benefits; see http://www.himss.org/asp/ContentRedirector.asp?ContentId=50254.

43 Bates DW, Leape LL, Cullen DJ, et al. Effect of computerized physician order entry and a team intervention on prevention of serious medication errors. *JAMA.* 1998;280:1311–1316.

44 Bates DW, Spell N, Cullen DJ, et al. The costs of adverse drug events in hospitalized patients. Adverse Drug Events Prevention Study Group. *JAMA.* 1997;277:307–311.

45 Johnston D, Pan E, et al. (2003). *The Value of Computerized Provider Order Entry in Ambulatory Settings.* Boston: Center for Information Technology Leadership; 2003.

46 Teich JM, Glaser JP, Beckley RF, et al. *Toward Cost-effective, Quality Care: The Brigham Integrated Computing System.* Proceedings Nicholas E. Davies CPR Recognition Symposium. New York: McGraw-Hill; 1996; 2:3–34.

47 See, for example: Dodd DW. The return of rigorous cost justification. *College Planning & Mgmt.* 2004; 7(2): 14; How to create a "tight" WMS cost justification proposal. *Inventory Mgmt Report.* 2003; July: 1.

Additional Web Reading and Resources

- Addressing medication errors in hospitals: a framework for developing a plan. http://www.chcf.org/topics/view.cfm?itemID=12682.

- Bates DW, Gawande AA. Patient safety: improving safety with information technology. *N Engl J Med.* 2003;384;25:2526–2534.

- Institute of Medicine (IOM) Reports

    - Patient Safety: Achieving a New Standard for Care (2003: http://www.iom.edu/report.asp?id=16663).

    - Key Capabilities of an Electronic Health Record System (2003: http://www.nap.edu/catalog/10781.html; see especially Decision Support Core Functionality, described on page 8).

    - Fostering Rapid Advances in Health Care: Learning from System Demonstrations (2002: http://www.iom.edu/report.asp?id=4294; e.g., see executive summary and Chapter 4 on Information and Communications Technology Infrastructure).

- Crossing the Quality Chasm: A New Health System for the 21st Century (2001: http://www.iom.edu/report.asp?id=5432).

- To Err Is Human: Building a Safer Health System (1999: http://www.iom.edu/report.asp?id=5575).

- Kuperman G, Gibson R. Computer physician order entry: benefits, costs, issues. *Ann Int Med.* 2003;139:31–39.

- Metzger J, Stablein D, Turisco F. Clinical Decision Support: Finding the Right Path. First Consulting Group First Reports. September 2002. https://www.fcg.com/research/serve-research.asp?rid=61 (registration and log-in required).

- Monographs of winning Davies Award submissions contain extensive information about how winners addressed people issues related to CIS and CDS implementation. http://www.himss.org/asp/davies_organizational.asp.

Chapter 2

Cataloging Available Information Systems

The clinical information systems (CIS) available within an organization, along with CDS-related features, need to be cataloged to identify the available tools that can be used to process and deliver CDS interventions and to determine what new tools may be necessary. When choosing the best interventions to achieve a given objective (see Chapter 3, page 41), you will draw from this catalog.

TASK

1. Prepare an inventory of your organization's clinical information systems that could play a role in delivering CDS interventions. For each system, note its pertinent CDS capabilities, coding systems, and current usage (Worksheet 2-1, page 37).

Key Lessons

- The data types and features provided in the major CIS applications that your organization has deployed help determine the types of CDS interventions that are available to you.

- Powerful CDS is dependent on a reliable, fast, and usable CIS **infrastructure**.

- Additional CIS features that impact CDS capabilities include availability of **coded data,** use of standard vocabularies, and ability to aggregate data from multiple sources.

- There are six major types of CDS interventions provided by CIS applications. Understanding these different types, and their advantages and disadvantages, is critical in selecting and designing optimal interventions to accomplish specific goals.

DISCUSSION
Which Came First ...

When you select interventions to meet clinical objectives in Chapter 3, you will see that the available interventions are determined by the CDS features provided in your core CIS applications. For some intervention types, such as certain alerts and reminders, the patient-specific data available in the EMR and related systems will also be a constraining factor. Thus, considering CDS targets as part of CIS procurement requirements can help ensure that, over time, the tools needed for optimal CDS effectiveness will be available. Strategic planning that involves IT and business and clinical leadership, and anticipates this interdependent relationship between CIS and CDS, can help the organization navigate the expensive and potentially risky challenge of CIS procurement and deployment. Of course, if your formal CDS program begins before core CIS **functionality** is in place, there initially might be less robust options for delivering CDS interventions.

In organizations where major CIS elements are already in place, the reverse is true. That is, initially there might be a broader range of workflow-integrated CDS options available, but there could be less flexibility in crafting the interventions to meet specific needs than there might be if a new information system were purchased and installed with those needs in mind.

Because technology infrastructure is a foundation for delivering CDS interventions, the IT department is often the initial home for CDS programs. This makes sense to the extent that the systems, staff, and budget pertinent to the program are managed there. However, the CDS program should be more than an IT project subsumed under CIS purchasing and implementation. As discussed in Chapter 1, the CDS program will be most effective in addressing priority goals if it is approached as a key strategic initiative, more clinical than IT, and is staffed and managed accordingly (e.g., taking into consideration the roles outlined in Figures 1-2 and 1-3). Helpful guides on clinical information systems implementation are available[1,2] and can be used in conjunction with this book to ensure that the CIS and CDS efforts are optimally effective and synergistic.

Core CIS Elements
Basic Information System Infrastructure

CDS capabilities depend not only on CIS application features but also on available hardware and software infrastructure. The performance of the computer network, availability of workstations, wireless coverage, system reliability, and similar features are important enablers (or impediments) for developing a powerful, usable **CDS system**. It is important, therefore, to assess the basic features and stability of your computing environment. Key elements to consider are outlined in Figure 2-1.[3]

Significant problems or limitations with these features in your environment might warrant attention early in CDS program planning to minimize problems later during implementation. For example, it would be unwise to begin developing CDS interventions that deliver knowledge over the network to clinicians via workstations if there are not adequate numbers of workstations conveniently available in prime locations that users can readily access. Similarly, those workstations and the network should be free from maintenance problems and unacceptable downtime.

You should also consider overall usability, that is, users' baseline interactions with the underlying hardware and software that will convey the CDS intervention. Users should be trained on effectively using these devices and programs, and any usability problems should be fixed before adding CDS interventions, since these problems will likely hinder successful CDS. Beyond just being able to successfully interact with the information systems, users should be comfortable with them to the greatest extent possible. Remember that individuals have a limited capacity for absorbing new skills and changes to routine. Adding new CDS-related tasks on top of shaky interactions with the underlying systems can undermine the success of both.

Figure 2-1: Information system infrastructure characteristics

Hardware/software	• *Number* of workstations/terminals, handheld/portable devices, printers, including per bed, per clinician • *Quality:* age, software/operating system version • *Reliability:* e.g., percent uptime, maintenance issues • *Performance:* speed of the core applications, as perceived by users
Network connectivity	• *Number* and proportion of computers connected to internet and high-speed internal communications
Wireless/remote systems	• *Number* and use of wireless devices: smart phones, wireless PDA, alphanumeric pager, wireless laptops • *Telemedicine* infrastructure (e.g., remote monitoring or data gathering from patients at home via machines that measure blood pressure and blood sugar) • *Remote access* to information systems by clinicians
Medical devices that generate patient data	• *Number* and *type* of medical instruments that gather and can deliver data about patients (e.g., electrocardiogram machines, automated blood pressure monitors)
Integration among clinical systems	• *Number* of different terminals/workstations/windows required to access the full portfolio of available applications

CIS Applications

CDS interventions are most effective when tightly integrated into workflow. Generally, this involves incorporating them into the clinical information systems that underpin patient care processes. Figure 2-2, page 28, lists a broad range of CIS that can serve as channels for delivering CDS interventions. Clinicians and patients interact directly with some of these systems, making them important conduits through which **CDS content** can be delivered. Other systems that might not be within typical clinician or patient workflow, such as scheduling or billing systems, can provide patient-related demographic information that will be used in CDS interventions. Most organizations have some applications that provide medical knowledge to clinicians and patients (e.g., via an intranet or the Internet). These should be considered in the survey as well. As you develop your catalog of information systems and available infrastructure (Worksheet 2-1, page 37), refer to this table to ensure that you have covered the full range of available tools and applications.

Below is a discussion of several aspects of how these systems manage information that will be important for their use in clinical decision support interventions. These aspects should be considered when selecting, acquiring, and installing pertinent CIS components.

Standard Vocabularies. A robust CDS program will likely involve a variety of specific interventions delivered via several different information systems or system components. Even a single intervention, such as a clinical alert, might require information from several systems (such as laboratory, pharmacy, or CPOE) and perhaps also from external electronic knowledge sources. Integrating the various components of CDS interventions, such as pertinent patient data and clinical knowledge, often requires a

Figure 2-2: CIS applications pertinent to CDS interventions

Departmental data management	• Pharmacy information system • Laboratory information system/results reporting system • Radiology information/results reporting system
Clinical records and patient management	• Electronic medical records: ambulatory, inpatient, for patients (i.e. **personal health record/PHR**) • Department-oriented (e.g., anesthesia, cardiology) • Care tracking systems: Emergency department, operating room • Medication administration and documentation
Ordering	• Computerized provider order entry • E-prescribing systems
Data aggregation	• **Data warehouse** • Clinical data repository • External and internal registries (e.g., disease-specific registries and government immunization registry)
Clinical content	• Reference/knowledge sources for clinicians • Health information for patients • Health risk assessment tools
Financial/ administrative	• Charge capture system • Billing system • Scheduling/registration system • Directories: physician on-call and coverage schedules and pager numbers, clinician and patient e-mail addresses

common underlying vocabulary and coding scheme, as well as a variety of other standards for data elements and inter-system communication. Appendix A, page 111, provides background information on standards and their role in CDS that might help you make sense of this complex and evolving topic.

Coded information can be helpful (or required) to allow for the unambiguous querying of patient data and knowledge sources that might be required by a CDS intervention. A robust vocabulary typically is more than just a controlled list of codes matched to their names. Instead, a structured vocab-

ulary provides relationships among the concepts and details about those concepts. This, in turn, permits automated aggregation of related data by the CDS system and intelligent interpretation of those data. For example, a drug vocabulary may contain a class or grouping that identifies all penicillin-like antibiotics for use in drug-allergy checking. It may also contain the manufactured dose forms to facilitate drug ordering in a CPOE system.

Universally accepted vocabularies related to CDS do not exist yet, but some consensus is beginning to emerge. For example, there are codes for

Figure 2-3: Some standard vocabularies pertinent to CDS

Vocabulary	Coverage
Systemized Nomenclature Of Medicine Clinical Terms (SNOMED-CT)	Multiple areas
International Classification of Diseases Clinical Modification (ICD-9-CM, ICD-10-CM)	Diagnoses
Current Procedural Terminology (CPT-4)	Procedures
Logical Observation Identifiers Names and Codes (LOINC)	Laboratory tests
Healthcare Common Procedure Coding System (HCPCS)	Supplies, non-physician services
Code on Dental Procedures and Nomenclature (CDT)	Procedures
National Drug Codes (NDC)	Drug: Names
RxNorm	Drugs: Names + dose forms
National Drug File-Reference Terminology (NDF-RT)	Drugs: Mechanism of action, physiologic effects
HIPAA code sets	Billing, administrative functions
Health Level Seven (HL7)	Multiple areas

medical and nursing diagnoses and procedures, laboratory and radiology tests, and medications. Many of these coding systems have been endorsed by various U.S. government agencies, including by units of the Department of Health and Human Services under its **Health Insurance Portability and Accountability Act (HIPAA)** authority, and by additional agencies cooperating under the **Consolidated Health Informatics** effort.[4] Figure 2-3 outlines vocabulary standards that are most relevant to CDS. Other standards are included in Appendix A.

The **Common Terminology Services (CTS)** standard of HL7 provides a standard for exchanging messages with a standard vocabulary in electronic format. Information systems can use the CTS standard, in combination with appropriate vocabularies, to translate from one code set to another and to look up a code given its name (and vice versa). Such translations can be important during execution

of a CDS intervention when a system is querying a repository for patient data.

Using consensus or standard vocabularies facilitates reporting of data to regulatory and accreditation agencies. It also allows exchange of data among organizations without the need to translate from one non-standard coding scheme to another. For example, a government agency may require your organization to report laboratory test results regarding HIV infection using LOINC codes. This allows the agency to aggregate data from many places and still understand what each data element means. If your laboratory does not use these codes, your personnel may have to translate your local codes into the LOINC standard before the agency will accept them as fulfilling regulations.

Coded data in your CIS can facilitate use of CDS interventions that use those same coding schemes to refer to data used by the **knowledge**

intervention. Even if standard codes are used, each healthcare organization may need to represent certain local concepts with codes not found in a standard vocabulary. These codes might include concepts unique to a local organization (such as physical locations referenced by the logic of an alert) or vendor-supplied codes in ancillary systems.

Keep these issues in mind as you consider what coding schemes are used in your CIS and how these might interplay with CDS interventions you may wish to deploy. If your systems do not use standard vocabularies and they are needed for a CDS intervention, one option is to work with the CIS vendor to convert or map them to standard schemes. Some healthcare organizations create a local vocabulary that maps local or CIS vendor codes to standard schemes. Whatever approach you take, it is important to maintain up-to-date information about the coding schemes used by all the pertinent CDS interventions and clinical information systems. During and after intervention deployment, it is also important to keep in mind that sources of coding schemes may abruptly reuse codes and thereby change their meaning and corresponding intervention behavior.

Other Standards. In addition to standard vocabularies, other standards are important for collection, transmission, and integration of data identified by these vocabularies. While incorporation of these standards into information systems in your organization is not absolutely required, their use increases the possibility of being able to exchange data and knowledge, such as rules with other organizations, or transmit data to regulatory or professional organizations without having to translate those data to another format. The most important of these are listed in Figure 2-4, while others are included in Appendix A.

Data Aggregation. Some healthcare organizations aggregate data from various ancillary systems or applications into a common database or repository. The way in which this is done can have implications for what types of CDS interventions may be delivered and how they are created.

When data is not aggregated, but instead distributed among various software applications, mechanisms for retrieving and combining the data will have to be explicitly developed for CDS interventions that require this disparate data. In this situation, you must determine whether the applications have modules that enable messaging or some sort of communication capability that provides access to needed data. The ease with which data can be exchanged will be determined, in part, by whether the access methods are compliant with any standard, such as a specific version of the HL7 messaging standard. In some cases, specific applications may have these modules, but they may not have been installed or activated at a particular location. Doing so may require additional cost or further negotiation with a vendor.

Even in those settings in which data may be aggregated continuously into a central **clinical data repository (CDR),** the properties of this repository will have an impact on the design of the CDS intervention. Key issues to consider include:

- What types of data are available?
- How quickly is the repository updated after data appears in the individual source systems?
- Does the repository make use of standard vocabularies (such as SNOMED-CT or LOINC), or are the data stored with their original vendor terminology?
- Is the CDR data organized so that needed data of a given type from all sources can be retrieved together?

Keep in mind that any changes in the vocabulary (for example, through the installation of a new laboratory information system) or the database organization may affect any CDS interventions that rely upon it. For example, the laboratory information system may store test results of kidney function (e.g., serum creatinine) using a particular code. To retrieve those results from the database to generate an alert for worsening kidney function, the CDS rule would be written to query all those results with that particular code. If the laboratory subsequently changed the code for the test,

Figure 2-4: Other standards pertinent to CDS or the systems from which the CDS system gathers data

Standard	Coverage
National Council of Prescription Drug Plans SCRIPT	Retail pharmacy transactions
IEEE 1073	Bedside device messaging
Digital Imaging and Communications in Medicine (DICOM)	Imaging data
ANSI X12	Claims/encounter data
Health Level Seven (HL7) messaging standard	Clinical data
Clinical Document Architecture (HL7 CDA)	Clinical reports
Clinical Context Object Workgroup (HL7 CCOW)	Desktop inter-application communication
Arden Syntax	Rules
Guideline Elements Model (GEM)	Clinical practice guidelines

the CDS system would be able to retrieve only old results and not more recent ones, thus rendering any processing of those data inaccurate. Therefore coordinating any such information system changes with CDS implementers is important.

Some organizations maintain a distinct data warehouse into which data are stored periodically, but not necessarily in real time. Data warehouses are often used by administrators for quality assurance and by researchers to perform scientific studies. While the data warehouse may not be as up-to-date as the clinical data repository at any given moment, the warehouse may be used for CDS when the interventions are not necessarily urgent or time-sensitive (e.g., to prepare a list of outpatients overdue for an indicated screening test). Using a data warehouse for this type of intervention can help reduce the processing load from CDS interventions on real-time information systems used for direct patient care.

Many larger organizations create registries of information about patients with chronic diseases to help manage these patients. Disease registries can be powerful assets for a CDS program because

they contain key information about the process and outcomes of care for clinical conditions that are the focus of performance improvement efforts. Like data warehouses, these registries can be used in CDS interventions alone or in combination with EMRs or other CIS (e.g., to provide data for alerts to clinicians about patient events requiring attention).

Data Types and Key Elements. The types of data each clinical information system manipulates also helps determine the role that the system can play in specific CDS interventions. Data types include:

- **Patient-centric,** such as medications, allergies, lab test results, imaging study results, visit history, health maintenance and immunization records, prior orders, problems, diagnoses, interventions and procedures, history and physical examination findings, and others.
- **Practice-centric** or **site-specific,** such as local antibiotic resistance patterns and sensitivities, formularies, referral lists, practice-specific "favorites" lists (e.g., for drug and test orders), and others.

Because they are such key drivers of care quality and cost-effectiveness, coded patient-centric data including problem lists, medication lists, and test results will figure prominently in your CDS interventions. These items deserve special attention in your information system survey.

Coded data about a patient's clinical findings can be useful triggers and inputs for CDS interventions. However, clinicians typically record subjective patient observations as uncoded data (commonly called "**free text**") that is difficult to use in CDS interventions. In some circumstances, automated coding systems can assign terms from a structured vocabulary to free text to facilitate processing by the intervention, although these are not common in current production systems.

CDS Intervention Types

To date, there are no widely accepted taxonomies of clinical decision support interventions, although there are published classifications of medical errors[5] and some discussions of CDS types.[6] We introduce a new taxonomy for a number of reasons. First and foremost, such a classification makes it much easier to identify the best type of intervention for meeting specific classes of clinical objectives (see Chapter 3), which is one of the primary purposes of this book.

Additionally, we hope that our taxonomy will make it easier to classify and apply research into CDS impact. Optimal use of CDS is still largely an art. While this book conveys many lessons of that art, more research is needed on the effectiveness of specific interventions to achieve specific objectives. We hope that the broad intervention classification and related discussions presented in this book will help organize the conduct, reporting, and application of such studies.

Figure 2-5 presents a categorized overview of CDS intervention types that is slightly modified from the version of the taxonomy in the first edition of this book.

Note that in practice, CDS interventions are often formed by combining these intervention types (such as by linking an alert to supporting reference materials).

These intervention types comprise the CDS option palette that can be used to address the clinical objectives identified in Chapter 1. We will link these more closely in Chapter 3. The specific interventions and functionality that are available to you will depend heavily on the CIS that you have in your environment to deliver them.

In the next chapter we will explore in great detail how to select specific interventions to accomplish individual objectives. For now, it will be useful to familiarize yourself with these intervention types so you can assess, in the following worksheet, which of these intervention types are available in your clinical information systems.

WORKSHEET

Step 1: Conduct and document an inventory of your organization's CIS that could play a role in delivering CDS interventions. For each system, note its pertinent CDS capabilities, coding systems and current usage.

The discussion above should help you survey the CIS applications in your organization to determine what information technology infrastructure is available to help you achieve the goals and objectives outlined in Chapter 1. Think broadly about what applications might be pertinent, using Figure 2-2, page 28, as a guide. Key executives or staff in your IT department can be a good starting point for gathering the information about the breadth and details of pertinent systems.

Include in your survey all the different clinical content and knowledge resources that are available in your organization to support clinical care and decision making. This might include content that has been developed locally, such as clinical protocols and guidelines, or content that is licensed from content vendors, such as clinical reference databases or knowledge components integrated into the CIS. While in most cases the information will be in electronic format and delivered via electronic clinical

Figure 2-5: Clinical decision support intervention types

1. Documentation forms/templates

Benefits: provide complete documentation for quality/continuity of care, reimbursement, legal; reduce errors of omission by displaying items for selection; provide coded data for other data-driven CDS

Subtypes	Examples
1.1 Patient self-assessment forms	Pre-visit questionnaires
	Health risk appraisals
1.2 Nursing patient assessment forms	Inpatient admission assessment
	Kardex
1.3 Clinician encounter documentation forms	Structured history and physical template
	Problem-specific assessment template
	Intelligent referral form
1.4 Departmental/multidisciplinary clinical documentation forms	Emergency department documentation
	Ambulatory care documentation
	Combinations of the above
1.5 Data flowsheets (usually a mixture of data entry form and relevant data display, see below)	Immunization flowsheet
	Health maintenance/disease management form
	Pay-for-performance (e.g., quality measure tracking) form

2. Relevant data presentation

Benefits: optimize decision making by ensuring all pertinent data are considered; organize complex data collections to promote understanding of overall picture and to highlight needed actions

Subtypes	Examples
2.1 Relevant data for ordering or documentation	Display of relevant lab tests when ordering a medication
	Display of current hematocrit and status of crossmatch when ordering blood products
2.2 Choice lists	Suggested dose choice lists, possibly modified by patient's renal function and age
	On-formulary display for a drug class
2.3 Practice status display	OR scheduling and status display
	Emergency department tracking display

Figure 2-5 *continued*

2.4 Retrospective/aggregate reporting or filtering

Physician practice audit and feedback

Physician "report cards"

List of all patients overdue for a key preventive care intervention

List of all patients in disease management program with abnormal results

2.5 Environmental parameter reporting

Recent hospital antibiotic sensitivities

3. Order creation facilitators

Benefits: Promote adherence to standards of care by making the right thing the easiest to do

Subtypes

Examples

3.1 Single-order completers including consequent orders

Prompts for appropriate orders and documentation (e.g., for specific sub-tests when ordering toxic screen), or for reasons when ordering certain tests

Suggested dose choice lists, possibly modified by patient's renal function and age

Consequent order suggestions (e.g., for drug levels when ordering certain antibiotics or pre-medication when ordering blood products)

3.2 **Order sets**

General order sets (e.g., for hospital admission)

Condition-specific order sets (e.g., for heart attack)

Post-op order sets

Order sets containing orders that are fully specified, contain parameter choices, have "fill-in-the-blank" fields, or a combination of the three

Active Guidelines[7]

3.3 Tools for complex ordering

Guided dose algorithms

TPN ordering forms with built-in calculators

4. Time-based checking and protocol/pathway support

Benefits: Provide support for multi-step care plans, pathways, and protocols that extend over time

Subtypes

Examples

4.1 Stepwise processing of multi-step protocol or guideline

Tools for monitoring and supporting inpatient clinical pathways (e.g., for pneumonia admissions) and multi-day chemotherapy protocols

4.2 Support for managing clinical problems over long periods and many encounters[8]

Computer-assisted management algorithm for treating hyperlipidemia over many outpatient visits

Figure 2-5 *continued*

5. Reference information and guidance

Benefits: Address recognized information needs of patients and clinicians

Subtypes	Examples
5.1 Context-insensitive	General link from EMR or clinical portal to a reference program (at table of contents or general-search level)
5.2 Context-sensitive	Direct links to specific, pertinent reference needed (via **infobuttons,**[9] **KnowledgeLinks**); e.g., link from medication order screen to display of side effects for that medication; link from problem-list entry to recent reviews of treatment for that problem
	Link from immunization flowsheet to table of standard immunization intervals
	Link in patient-messaging application to relevant patient information leaflets
	Calculators/nomograms
	Diagnostic decision support driven by patient-specific data

6. Reactive alerts and reminders (i.e., unsolicited by patient or clinician recipient)

Benefits: Provide immediate notification of errors and hazards related to new data or orders entered by CIS user or the CIS itself (e.g., when abnormal lab result is posted), or passage of a time interval during which a critical event should occur; help enforce standards of care

Subtypes	Examples
6.1 Alerts to prevent potential errors or hazards	Drug allergy alert
	Drug interaction alert (e.g., with drugs, food)
	Under/overdose alert (single dose, total dose, frequency, etc.; general or specific for age, weight, laboratory results)
	Wrong drug route alert
	Patient specific contraindication for clinical intervention
	Inappropriate therapeutic duplication or medication administration route
	Incorrect test or study for an indication or inappropriate testing interval
	Critical lab test result notification
	User-requested notification when lab result is available or other key event has occurred

---

Figure 2-5 *continued*

6.2 Alerts to foster best care	Disease management (e.g., alert for needed therapeutic intervention)
	Medication order triggers display of more cost-effective drug, regimen or formulary-compliant option
	Wellness management (e.g., alert for patient needing flu shot)
	Reminder to document patient smoking status and provide counseling as needed
	Suggestion to add patient to a study or protocol

---

information systems, remember that paper-based CDS interventions (e.g., relevant data summaries, order sets) can be effective[10] and may have a role in your program.

Your organization's clinical knowledge resources provide an initial content base for achieving the clinical goals within the CDS program. Some of these assets might be stand-alone reference databases, while others might be tightly integrated into specific clinical systems (for example, drug interaction detection within CPOE). Additional content (developed locally, shared with other institutions, or acquired from CIS or content vendors) may be required to optimally address the CDS program goals. The **knowledge asset** survey provides a foundation for making this assessment in Chapter 3.

In addition to documenting systems already in place, Worksheet 2-1 can be used to record information about specific systems you are considering adding. This can help clarify how new components might enhance your IT infrastructure for CDS.

Worksheet 2-1:

CIS inventory

In the first column of this worksheet, list the name and system type (e.g., from Figure 2-2) for all the CIS components that you have identified in your survey. If the number of available systems is large, you might initially focus on the systems that appear most pertinent and powerful to achieve your clinical objectives. Keep in mind that the more comprehensively you outline your infrastructure, the easier it will be to identify potential CDS intervention options that are available in your environment.

In the second column, begin noting which of the CDS intervention types from Figure 2-5, page 33, that each system can deliver or facilitate. You might need to refine this section as you get into more intervention development details in the next chapter.

This book emphasizes the importance of data in coded form for use in CDS interventions. In the third column, document the types of information the system handles and any coding schemes used. Again, pay particular attention to key items, such as laboratory test names, drug names, and patients' clinical problems.

In Chapter 3, we will explore in detail how to reach CDS recipients in their workflow. The fourth worksheet column provides a foundation for this by characterizing the types of system users and the penetration of that system into that user population. The notes column can be used to document other key system features such as any knowledge bases it contains and its interoperability with other key systems.

System Name/ Type	CDS-related Functionality	Information Types (Coding System)	System Users and Usage	Notes
Ordering				
See clinical records, below				
Clinical records and patient management				
Better Care Inc./ Inpatient EMR	• Order sets • Documentation templates • Relevant data display • Alerts	• Diagnosis information (ICD10) • Order information (CPT) • Lab results (LOINC) • Imaging results (home-grown scheme)	Nurses, doctors, and pharmacists. 100% of physicians are currently using	Uses drug knowledge base from XYZ Corp for drug interaction and allergy alerting
Outpatient Computer Corp.	• Order sets • Documentation templates • Relevant data display • Alerts	• Visit diagnosis (ICD10) • Problem lists (ICD10) • Medication lists (NDC) • Visit notes (Text)	25% of outpatient clinics, mostly primary care	Not yet exchanging data well with inpatient system

Worksheet 2-1 *continued*

System Name/ Type	CDS-related Functionality	Information Types (Coding System)	System Users and Usage	Notes
Given Meds Corp.	• Alerts • Documentation templates • Relevant data display	• Date/time for medication administration • Medications (NDC) • Dose administered	100% of nurses at two hospitals	Linked to handheld devices
Departmental data management				
Get your labs inc.	• Relevant data display • Alerts	• Lab results (LOINC) • Anatomic pathology results (Text)	Doctors, nurses, pharmacists all use it frequently	
Clinical content				
Know-it-all Reference	• Disease and drug reference—infobutton capability	• Disease management info (ICD-9) • Drug reference info (NDC)	Doctors, nurses, pharmacists all use it frequently	Linked to handheld devices
Data aggregation				
N/A				

CONCLUDING COMMENTS

After completing Worksheet 2-1, you should have a very detailed and useful picture of the information systems and CDS-related content currently available in your organization. This infrastructure will support the CDS interventions needed to meet the goals and objectives you defined in Chapter 1.

In many cases, your organization will not have all the infrastructure, functionality, and interoperability that you would want in order to achieve all your goals and objectives. Although the current CIS portfolio might limit the opportunities to select specific CDS interventions, your analysis in this section will help you make the best use of available infrastructure. In addition, this documentation can help set the stage for business cases that define the need for enhancements to IT infrastructure that could more fully meet organizational needs.

The next chapter discusses how to select specific CDS interventions that will leverage current information systems to achieve CDS program targets. The assessment of supported data types and vocabularies foreshadows logistical considerations that might arise from trying to coordinate information flow in potentially disparate systems.

References

1 Blander J, Bergeron BP. *Clinical Management Systems: A Guide for Deployment.* Chicago: HIMSS; 2004.

2 Miller J (ed). *Implementing the Electronic Health Record: Case Studies and Lessons Learned.* Chicago: HIMSS; 2005.

3 The HIMSS CIS Benefits Realization Task Force is developing an evaluation tool to assess the level of clinical information system infusion in an organization (http://www.himss.org/asp/committees_ehr.asp#5). The tool provides a quantitative assessment of the items outlined in this table and an overall score indicating the aggregate level of CIS infusion. A version of this scoring system can be found at: Leonard KA, Sittig DF. Does measurement improve performance? First IMPROVE-IT Conference, Toronto, CA November 2004 (http://www.improve-it-institute.org/First_Conf_White.pdf): 20.

4 http://www.whitehouse.gov/omb/egov/c-3-6-chi.html.

5 Dovey SM, Phillips RL, Green LA, Fryer GE. Types of medical errors commonly reported by family physicians. *Am Fam Physician.* 2003;67:697.

6 Teich JM. Inpatient order management. *JHIM.* 1999; 13(2):97–111.

7 Tang PC, Young CY. ActiveGuidelines: integrating Web-based guidelines with computer-based patient records. *AMIA Proceedings.* 2000;843–7.

8 Maviglia SM et al. Automating complex guidelines for chronic disease: lessons learned. *JAMIA.* 10:154–165 (2003).

9 Academic institutions have been developing, deploying, and evaluating infobuttons (providing context-sensitive links to reference material from within a CIS—called KnowledgeLink in some institutions) for several years. HL7 is developing a standard for this approach. CDS content vendors and CIS vendors are participating in this standard development and are also releasing initial commercial products into the marketplace in advance of the formal standard specification.

10 Montgomery AA, et al. Evaluation of computer based clinical decision support system and risk chart for management of hypertension in primary care: randomised controlled trial. *BMJ.* 2000; 320:(7236):686–90.

Additional Web Reading and Resources

- Health Level Seven **Electronic Health Record** Functional Model and Standard: http://www.hl7.org/ehr/; this model and standard will include descriptions of clinical decision support functions within EMRs.* See also the **EHR** Collaborative Web site: http://www.ehrcollaborative.org/.

- Healthcare Informatics Annual Resource Guide (http://www.healthcare-informatics.com/aresource.htm) lists many commercial clinical information systems.

---

* There is no widely accepted understanding of the difference between EHR and EMR. In this book, we use EMR because it has traditionally been the most common term used to describe these systems.

Chapter 3

Selecting and Specifying CDS Interventions

In the previous two chapters, you established the CDS targets that your organization hopes to achieve and surveyed the information system capabilities available to achieve them. This chapter will help you select the most effective CDS interventions to realize each specific objective.

TASKS

1. Assign an **objective class** to each clinical objective for which you are developing a CDS intervention (Worksheet 3-1, page 67).

2. Use the objective classes to help identify optimal CDS interventions and workflow opportunities for addressing each corresponding objective, given the capabilities of your available clinical information systems (Worksheet 3-1, page 67).

Key Lessons

- Clinical objectives can be classified into objective classes. Different objective classes are optimally addressed by a subset of the full spectrum of CDS intervention types. Categorizing objectives into classes can therefore help determine the best intervention to meet a particular need (Figure 3-1, page 43, and Figure 3-3, page 46).

- Similarly, different interventions are most effective for achieving specific objectives when delivered at specific points in clinical workflow (Figure 3-2, page 45, and Figure 3-3).

- The final selection of the best intervention(s) to meet a particular need is based on specific selection factors reflecting availability of the intervention in your CIS (from Chapter 2), ease of implementation, acceptability, and impact of each type of intervention (Figure 3-4, page 57).

- Careful attention is required to benefits realization during intervention selection and implementation. It is essential to remain sharply focused on the quantified care improvement that is expected and ensure that the emerging interventions will deliver this benefit and enable its measurement.

DISCUSSION

The inventory of local CIS and their CDS capabilities establishes the universe of available CDS tools and interventions. The next step is to review and classify each clinical objective from Chapter 1 and then to determine what specific CDS interventions will be able to best accomplish each objective.

The key questions we will answer in this chapter to help accomplish this are:

- *What* groupings or classes of objectives can be helpful in creating a link between specific objectives and useful interventions?
- *When* in the process of care are the most effective times to deliver interventions directed toward a specific objective class?
- *What types* of CDS interventions are effective in addressing a given class of clinical objective? Drilling down further, which specific intervention types will be most useful for this specific objective?

The following discussion addresses each of these questions in turn.

Clinical Objective Classes

Most clinical objectives can be grouped into a few specific classes, where each class lends itself to specific types of CDS interventions. For example, there is a family of clinical objectives that involves ensuring that relatively simple and discrete care guidelines are followed, such as increasing the proportion of eligible patients who have regular cholesterol screening. Interventions that effectively address this specific objective can also be useful for other objectives in the same class, such as providing regular mammograms. CDS interventions useful across this entire class of objectives include flowsheets that help remind clinicians when the intervention was performed, order sets that help ensure appropriate ordering, and alerts that remind clinicians when the intervention is overdue.

Mapping specific clinical objectives to objective classes, mapping those classes to CDS opportunity points in workflow, and then selecting specific CDS interventions pertinent to the CDS opportunity points can help you find the best interventions to achieve those objectives. Figure 3-1 illustrates the first link in this chain by outlining classes of clinical objectives and examples of each.

Workflow Opportunities: Optimal Timing of CDS

In the clinician and patient workflow, it is important to consider *when* are the most effective times to deliver CDS interventions. Different objective classes are best addressed with CDS interventions at different points in this workflow. The best opportunity is usually when

- Pertinent clinical data becomes available;
- Pertinent persons can be reached with the intervention; and
- Those persons are prepared to act upon the information immediately.

These opportunities can be spread across healthcare system encounters, such as ambulatory or emergency department visits, and inpatient admissions. The opportunities can arise at variety of points within an encounter, such as at pre-visit, patient intake and clinician documentation, ordering, and results review. Sometimes, the best opportunity occurs outside of any encounter, such as when test results are posted after an encounter or when a patient is performing self-care and home monitoring.

Figure 3-2, page 45, diagrams the general process of healthcare workflow for inpatient and ambulatory care. For CDS purposes, you can see that there are many parallels between inpatient and ambulatory workflow; these settings share common care processes where the same type of intervention may be effectively applied. The figure also shows a few examples of where in the workflow some specific CDS interventions are normally most effective. The workflow steps in Figure 3-2 will reappear in Figure 3-3, page 46, which indicates, for each clinical objective class, the optimal intervention types, and opportunities in the workflow.

Figure 3-1: Classes of objectives and specific examples*

OBJECTIVE CLASS	EXAMPLES
Prevent Errors	
Prevent errors of commission	• Decrease likelihood of prescribing an overdose of warfarin for patients with liver disease
	• Prevent allergic reactions, drug interactions and inappropriate therapeutic duplication in medication orders
	• Reduce inappropriate repetition of tests
	• Prevent medication overdose in patient requiring reduced dosages due to kidney disease
Prevent errors of omission	• Reduce inattention to critical lab values and other test results
	• Avoid missed steps in a necessary sequence, such as monitoring lab tests when certain drugs are ordered
	• Treat patients more rapidly once a condition or problem becomes apparent
Optimize Decision Making	
Optimize choice of *individual* tests and therapies based on additional considerations (such as cost-effectiveness)	• Improve compliance with on-formulary medications
	• Improve likelihood that less expensive anti-emetics are chosen over more expensive ones, when appropriate
Improve compliance with simple care guidelines (e.g., preventive services)	• Annual cholesterol/LDL testing performed for appropriate persons
	• Flu shots administered to appropriate persons
	• Clinicians order mammograms based on consensus guideline
Improve appropriateness of overall workup and treatment plan for a given situation	• Full complement of indicated interventions ordered for patients seen in the emergency department with acute MI
	• Most effective and efficient diagnostic evaluation ordered in ambulatory settings for patients with suspected rheumatologic disease
	• Improve appropriateness of referrals for abnormal Pap smears

* This figure will be further refined and expanded over time
with input from users of this guide.

Figure 3-1 *(continued)*

Improve compliance with complex short-term *multi-step protocols*	• Clinical pathway followed to minimize length of stay for a surgical admission for cholecystitis
	• Improve decision making and management of chemotherapy protocols
Optimize treatment of chronic conditions *over time* (for individuals and populations of patients); long-term management	• Improve hemoglobin A1c values in diabetics (individually and population-wide) over time
	• Improve management of asthma with inhaled steroids
Improve Care Processes	
Improve documentation of care, including eliciting key data from history and physical examination	• Improve likelihood of documenting patient allergy on nursing assessment
	• Assess and document patient smoking status at every encounter
	• Faster, more complete documentation of periodic encounter for diabetic patients, including foot examinations
Improve patient education, empowerment and satisfaction with care	• Promote appropriate patient understanding and self-management of specific conditions
	• Improve communication to patients about upcoming admissions and procedures
Improve communication among caregivers	• Increase sharing of patient-related data among caregivers (e.g., improved completeness and timeliness of patient history available to a consultant seeing a patient for the first time)

CDS can often be very effectively delivered to patients themselves, adding a powerful tool for fully engaging patients in their own care between health system encounters. Liberal use of interventions that empower patients (e.g., reminders to patients to obtain needed preventive care screening or immunizations, or tools to help them track and optimize critical disease markers) can help ensure that patients participate fully in achieving clinical objectives.

Interventions can be delivered to patients by high-tech means (e.g., via alerts in their personal health record or automated phone calls) or low-tech means (e.g., post cards), depending on their computer use and comfort with technology. Multipronged interventions working toward the same objective, delivered to clinicians/staff and also to patients (such as combining clinical flowsheets and patient reminders for indicated mammograms or flu shots) can be particularly effective.

Mapping Objective Classes to Possible Intervention Types

Figure 3-3 is a detailed framework for mapping clinical objectives to CDS intervention types that

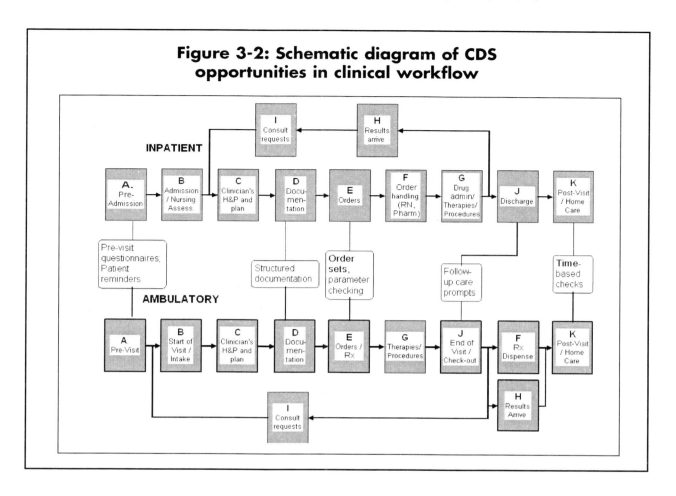

Figure 3-2: Schematic diagram of CDS opportunities in clinical workflow

can be applied at particular stages in the workflow.[1] As such, it is a linchpin for selecting CDS interventions to accomplish your objectives. Keep in mind that this mapping is an inexact science at present; research data underpinning these recommendations are scant at best. Nonetheless, Figure 3-3 provides a foundation for identifying the most effective CDS options and workflow opportunities for a given need.

Deciding Among Several Available Intervention Types
Selection Factors
Each objective class in Figure 3-3 maps to several different intervention types and points in workflow. Even after ruling out interventions that are not available in your environment, there may still be a number of options available.

The analysis of care process issues discussed on page 20 of Chapter 1 comes into play again here. That analysis should point to places in workflow where breakdowns occur and where there are opportunities for process improvement. If you can identify the steps in the care process where improvement is most needed, then corrective knowledge interventions at those particular steps might be particularly helpful for improving overall performance for the clinical objective of interest.

Say, for example, that improving ordering of periodic preventive care screening tests, such as mammograms, is a clinical objective in an organization due to a performance measurement program in this area. If these tests are completed at much lower rates than are appropriate, and process analysis determines that difficulty accessing information about the last time the patient had the test is a

Figure 3-3: Objective classes and workflow opportunities

PREVENT ERRORS

Objective Class	CDS Intervention Type	Workflow Step
Prevent errors of commission	**Alerts to prevent errors (6.1)*** Drug dosing, wrong route, drug allergies, duplicate orders, drug-drug, drug-food	Ordering (E)† Order handling (F) Therapies (G) Results arrive (H)
	Relevant data for ordering (2.1) Supply important data such as relevant lab tests that may affect the correctness of an order	Ordering (E) Results arrive (H)
	Choice lists (2.2) Prevent against erroneous doses, parameters, choice combinations	Documentation (D) Ordering (E)
	Single-order completers (3.1) Appropriate monitoring for potentially harmful drugs; appropriate reasons for tests	Ordering (E) Order handling ((F) Results arrive (H)
	Support for complex ordering and calculations (3.3) For complex dosing or administration regimens	Ordering (E) Medication administration (G)
	Flowsheets (1.5) Show important information for decision making	Start of visit/Admission (B) Clinician H&P (C) Documentation (D) Ordering (E)

Errors of commission occur when an action taken is incorrect for some reason. In the complex modern hospital and office, this most often means that the clinician was unaware of the potential danger of the action or has not taken into account some key piece of data in his or her decision making. Flowsheets are a good way to present information and decrease likelihood that key information will be missed. Alerts are the classic way of bringing the provider's attention to an impending error.

---

* The numbers in the second column correspond to the numbers in the table of intervention types (Figure 2-5).

† The letters in the third column correspond to the letters in Figure 3-2.

Figure 3-3 *continued*

Objective Class	CDS Intervention Type	Workflow Step
Prevent errors of omission	Order sets (3.2)	Ordering (E)
	Single-order completers and consequent orders (3.1)	Ordering (E)
		Therapies (G)
		Results arrive (H)
	Clinician encounter documentation forms (1.3)	Documentation (D)
	Nursing assessment forms (1.2)	Documentation (D)
	Practice status display (2.3)	Pre-visit (A)
	Heads up display to show missing tasks, prevent overlooked data	Start of visit (B)
		Order handling (F)
		Results arrive (H)
		Discharge (J)
	Alerts to foster best care (6.2)	Ordering (E)
		Therapies (G)
		Results arrive (H)
	Multistep protocol support/Clinical pathways (4.1)	Documentation (D)
	Improve the likelihood that a particular action will be well timed with others to prevent errors	Ordering (E)
		Therapies (G)

As used in this guide, errors of omission are defined to occur when a needed test or therapy is not prescribed for a patient. They generally include omissions of important follow-on steps in a sequence that has partly begun. This might include failure to check drug levels as indicated when a drug is ordered, or failure to renew a needed medication. (The separate class of keeping care consistent with recommended guidelines is handled in the next section.) The best way to avoid this type of error is to make the clinician aware of the needed action as soon as possible and to make it easy for the clinician to perform. Order sets, consequent orders, and patient-status displays may be the most effective ways of achieving this goal. Alerts that catch the problem after it has occurred are often a less efficient approach.

Figure 3-3 *continued*

OPTIMIZE DECISION MAKING

Objective Class	CDS Intervention Type	Workflow Step
Optimize choice of *individual* tests and therapies based on additional considerations (such as cost-effectiveness)	Order sets (3.2) Choice lists (2.2) Head off inappropriate choices before they are made	Ordering (E)
	Alerts to foster best care (6.2) Alerts regarding formulary violations, more cost-effective choices	Ordering (E)
	Consequent orders (3.1) Facilitating the more inexpensive order or appropriate referral	Ordering (E)
	Reference material (5) Tailored, highly specific reference about the various choices available	Ordering (E) Results arrive (H)

Here, the user is initiating a specific action, such as ordering antibiotics or referring a patient for consultation for a specific problem, and CDS is used to optimize the specific choices and parameters. The intervention is most convenient when presented proactively, in an order set or choice list, rather than correctively after one choice has already been made. For example, the system could present a choice list of antibiotics, in which each choice is accompanied by an indicator about its formulary status and its antibiotic sensitivity from culture results.

Figure 3-3 *continued*

Objective Class	CDS Intervention Type	Workflow Step
Improve compliance with simple care guidelines (e.g., health maintenance and preventive-care items)	Clinical data flowsheets (1.5) Showing screening tests over time; includes disease registry tools and forms	Start of visit (B) Documentation (D) Ordering (E) Discharge (J) Results arrive (H)
	Alerts and reminders to foster best care (6.2) Reminders for needed items	Ordering (E)
	Order sets (3.2) Containing the appropriate interventions based on patient risk	Ordering (E)
	Multidisciplinary (1.4) documentation forms	Documentation (D)
	Clinician encounter forms (1.3)	Documentation (D)
	Patient self-assessment forms (1.1) Health maintenance questionnaires	Pre-encounter (A) Office check-in (B)
	Reference information (context-sensitive preferred) (5.2) Showing screening/prevention recommendations based on diagnoses on the problem list	Pre-visit (A) Clinician H&P (C) Ordering (E) End of visit (J)

Simple care guidelines are typically easiest to facilitate during the ordering phase, although an important adjunct is to ensure that the provider is made aware of needed or recommended actions at the start of an encounter. Alerts and order sets are the strongest considerations for generating action. Documentation forms, flow sheets, order sets, and reference information are strong considerations for increasing awareness.

Figure 3-3 *continued*

Objective Class	CDS Intervention Type	Workflow Step
Optimize treatment of chronic conditions over time (long-term management)	Flowsheets (1.5) Showing indicators of disease severity and improvements over time	Intake/nursing assessment (B) Clinician H&P (C) Documentation (D) Ordering (E)
	Alerts to foster optimal care (6.2) Time based alerts are particularly relevant to chronic illness. Can be used to prompt attention to a protocol when significant events occur, e.g., new test results; also can identify patients with acute needs from a large population on a protocol	Ordering (E) Results arrive (H) Post-visit/home care (K)
	Aggregate reporting (2.4) Identify patients with acute needs or those who are falling off the protocol	Post-visit (K) Pre-visit (A)
	Order sets (3.2) Used to break up a long-term protocol into several discrete steps, then optimize handling of each step	Ordering (E)
	Patient self-assessment forms (1.1) Allow the patient to review his/her own status of chronic conditions, and to document them for use by (or alerts to) care providers	Pre-visit (A) Start of Visit (B) Post-visit (K)
	Reference material (5) General information directed at patients as well as clinicians. May be context-sensitive or insensitive in this usage	Pre-visit (A) Start of visit (B) Documentation (D) Ordering (E) Results arrive (H) Post-visit/Home care (K)
	Multi-step protocol support/Clinical pathways (4.1) Follow the steps of a long-term management algorithm; often these are presented to the user as alerts and flowsheets	Start of visit (B) Ordering (E) Results arrive (H)

Figure 3-3 continued

The care of chronic medical conditions often requires dealing with diverse data and indicated interventions that unfold over prolonged time periods. Interventions, such as flow sheets and order sets, can facilitate appropriate action in these patients. They work by breaking up a long-term management guideline into manageable steps, exposing and providing information about the relevant step, and prompting for action. Involving the patient is particularly important in the management of these conditions since many changes happen at home between encounters. Thus, patient self-assessment forms and reference information are important here. Surveillance systems can monitor hundreds or thousands of patients, review new data coming in, identify those patients whose data brings cause for concern, and use alerts to notify providers or care managers about such patients.

Figure 3-3 *continued*

Objective Class	CDS Intervention Type	Workflow Step
Improve appropriateness of *overall* workup and treatment plan for a given situation (e.g., best management steps for acute MI in the ED)	Reference information (context-sensitive) (5.2) Display the appropriate management information summary at the moment when it is needed	Start of visit (B) Documentation (D) Ordering (E) Order handling (F) Therapies (G) End of Visit (J) Post-visit/Home care (K)
	Order sets (3.2) Defined workup codified into an order set	Ordering (E)
	Flowsheets (1.5) Clinician documentation forms (1.3) Structured documentation forms prompt attention to necessary elements	Documentation (D) Clinician H&P (C) Discharge (J)
	Alerts to foster care plan (6.2)	Start of visit (B) Ordering (E) Results arrive (H)
	Aggregate reports (2.4) Showing prescribing patterns and referral patterns	Post-visit (K)
	Clinical pathways (4)	Documentation (D) Ordering (E)

One of the most important CDS functions is presenting a quick guide to managing the current acute situation. Reference information, especially when highly specific to the situation and when automatically presented, is low-tech but highly useful. Order sets that present a standard approach to management are also highly effective in these situations.

Figure 3-3 *continued*

Objective Class	CDS Intervention Type	Workflow Step
Improve compliance with clinical pathways, complex multistep protocols, and other very specific multistep protocols	Clinical pathways (4) They are a good way to optimize inpatient therapy over the course of a hospitalization	All points in the workflow
	Alerts (6) Both to foster best care and prevent errors that arise in complicated situations; reminders when next step is needed	Orders (E) Results Arrive (H)
	Multidisciplinary documentation forms (1.4)	Documentation (D)
	Order Sets (3.2) Can be used to specify orders for a given subset of the protocol, e.g., "Bone marrow transplant day 3 orders"	Orders (E) Results arrive (H)

Clinical pathways are the primary tool for optimizing complex multistep treatment protocols. But they are often more simply presented to the user as order sets and documentation forms that reflect a single major step in the complicated process.

Figure 3-3 *continued*

IMPROVE CARE PROCESSES

A full account of all care processes and how one might optimize them is beyond the scope of this table; below are some examples where knowledge interventions can be linked to specific care processes.

Objective Class	CDS Intervention Type	Workflow Step
Improve documentation	Nursing assessment forms (1.2) Clinician documentation forms (1.3) Intelligent documentation support ensures that key items aren't missed and that workups are complete	Documentation (D)
	Patient Self assessment forms (1.1) Structured forms, and forms with interactive prompts, can ensure that documentation is complete and sensitive to the patient's specific conditions and problems	Pre-encounter (A) Hospital admission/Start of visit (B) Post-visit (K)
	Multidisciplinary Forms (1.4) Promote communication among co-workers as well as reducing redundancy	Documentation (D)

Improving documentation is a very important component of working toward the complete EMR. It can be facilitated using all of the documentation types. From a CDS perspective, the emphasis is on moderately intelligent documentation tools, which guide the user to more complete documentation (and, as a consequence, a more thorough evaluation) of a given situation.

Figure 3-3 *continued*

Objective Class	CDS Intervention Type	Workflow Step
Improve patient education and empowerment	Patient self-assessment forms (1.1)	Pre-visit (A) Start of visit (B) Post-visit (K)
	Relevant data display (2.1) Multidisciplinary documentation forms (1.4) Discharge summary or visit summary information, and discharge medication summary sheets	Discharge (J)
	Alerts to foster better care (6.2) Alerts can be delivered to patients via personal health records, or an e-mail or postal letter about needed interventions or screening	Pre-visit (A) Post-visit (K)
	Order Sets (3.2) Can be used to trigger printout or display of information for distribution to patients and patient education	Start of visit/Admission (B) Documentation (D) Ordering (E) Discharge (J)
	Reference Information (context-sensitive) (5.2) In particular, for new drugs that are pre-scribed, and new diagnoses	Pre-visit (A) Start of visit (B) Orders (E) Order handling (F) Discharge (J)

Patients play a role in almost all of the workflow steps described in this chapter. This objective class refers to the use of knowledge interventions presented directly to patients themselves. While alerts delivered via interactive personal health records may be an attractive way of automatically communicating with patients, well-placed reference information is probably still the best approach to patient education. Direct sharing of data between personal and clinical health records is still at an experimental stage, due to technological and confidentiality considerations.

Figure 3-3 *continued*

Objective Class	CDS Intervention Type	Workflow Step
Improve communication among caregivers	Multidisciplinary documentation forms (1.4) Clinician documentation forms (1.3) Ensure that referrers and consultants both give the other the information they need	Documentation (D) Consult requests (I) Discharge (J)
	Alerts to foster best care (6.2) Reminder that patient is part of a referral; alert to new data arriving on referred patient	Therapies/Procedures (G) Results arrive (H) Post-visit (K)
	Multi-step protocol support (4.1) Allows all workers to see the current stage of the protocol	Documentation (D) Start of visit (B) Post-visit (K)

Primary aids to communication include complete, portable documentation forms, easy person-to-person messaging, and notification when a co-worker has performed significant actions on the patient.

major contributing factor, than a flowsheet with this information could be a useful intervention. On the other hand, if a process analysis is not done, and it is simply assumed that the process breakdown is at the physician ordering stage when in fact the problem is at the patient adherence stage, then there is a risk of developing interventions that will not be effective. In this case, alerts and flowsheets for the physician probably won't be helpful for driving the desired result, whereas CDS interventions directed toward the patient would likely be much more useful. Thus, careful examination of the processes that underlie outcomes targeted for improvement can help determine the CDS interventions and recipients that will be most productive.

After factoring in available CDS capabilities, care process weak points, and the general guidance from Figure 3-3 about promising CDS opportunities, the final choice of which intervention(s) to use in addressing a specific need depends on several factors, including:

- **Ease of development:** how hard or easy it is to develop the intervention;
- **Acceptability:** likelihood of the intervention being accepted by the intended decision makers;
- **Impact:** likelihood of the intervention leading to the desired effect; and
- **Special considerations** about each intervention type may make some types more or less desirable.

Figure 3-4 explores these selection factors for each intervention type outlined in Figure 2-5. It uses the definitions shown on the next page.

As noted above, Figures 3-3 and 3-4 (and the objectives classes in Figure 3-1) are based largely on expert opinion rather than extensive science. We welcome your feedback on improving these tools.

Definition of Terms Used in Figure 3-4

Ease of Development	How much time will it take to develop the structure and content of the intervention? How much special skill is needed to produce it?
Easy:	No programming knowledge necessary, requisite data is clear-cut and easily available
Moderate:	Low level programming knowledge, moderately complex to integrate into the system, weeks to months to build and test
Difficult:	Complex programming or database knowledge typically needed; logic, presentation, or actions may be complex or nonstandard
Acceptability	How likely is your user community to adopt this intervention?
High:	Highly acceptable: knowledge is non-controversial, easy to use, doesn't slow user down
Medium:	Knowledge is more difficult to accept or user may be slowed slightly
Low:	Knowledge is difficult to accept or user will be significantly slowed
Impact	Assuming the intervention is accepted by users, how likely is the intervention to create the intended effect?
Strong:	Over 75% chance of creating the intended effect. Usually interventions that provide easy access to direct, straightforward action
Moderate:	25–75% chance of creating the intended effect
Weak:	Expect 25% or lower chance of creating the intended effect

Figure 3-4: Selection factors

I. Documentation Forms

A. Ease of development (+ + +):

1. General ease: Moderate or Difficult depending on the complexity of form.

2. Specifications are often easy to come by because of pre-existing paper documentation forms used in many hospitals and clinics.

3. If you seek structured, machine-usable output from the form (e.g., evaluation and management codes for billing), then the form elements must be mapped to standard dictionaries, which can be difficult.

4. Making the form easy to use can be difficult, particularly for large forms.

Key: + (poor), + + (average), + + + (good)

Figure 3-4 *continued*

B. Acceptability (+):

   1. Low: Structured documentation forms are among the most difficult interventions to get users to use. Expect less than 25% compliance.

   2. More acceptable forms are those used for specific activities that are very repeatable, such as a normal pregnancy visit or focused eye exam.

C. Impact (+ +):

   1. Moderate: If properly developed and accepted, such forms create readable, findable documentation and have a reasonable likelihood of producing the intended data and calculations.

D. Special considerations:

   1. Be sure to plan an organized method for naming and numbering elements on your documentation forms. This will make it easier for users to find them in your system and to use the data when you create reports and other decision support interventions such as alerts.

   2. Personal (unvetted) forms are controversial, as they can lead to a large amount of difficult-to-control content.

E. Examples and subtypes:

   1. Nursing assessment forms

      a) These are among the more acceptable forms because of the high degree of structure in inpatient nursing assessments, particularly the admission assessment.

   2. Encounter documentation forms

      a) A single form can be used for all of an encounter or several modules can be combined in one encounter (e.g., an additional form can be used to document functional status for patients with arthritis)

      b) Excellent place to embed other CDS, such as relevant data display and reference material.

   3. Patient self-assessment forms

      a) Acceptability depends highly on providing easy access to these forms, tying them to a direct patient benefit (such as quicker service), and paying great attention to usability and readability.

      b) As with all patient interventions, attention must be given to variations in language and word usage.

      c) Patient forms can include data previously entered by providers, and vice-versa. However, data ownership, privacy and confidentiality must be carefully protected.

   4. Multidisciplinary forms

      a) Different elements of the form can be completed by different clinicians, while all can view each other's entries. A good means of coordinating workflow across multiple provider types; particularly useful in emergency medicine and for the hospital discharge process.

Key: + (poor), + + (average), + + + (good)

Figure 3-4 *continued*

II. Relevant Data Display

A. Ease of development (+ +):

1. Moderate: Retrieving the correct patient information and displaying it at the appropriate moment (e.g., on an ordering form) can require nonstandard programming.

2. Difficulty is increased when the relevant data elements can come from multiple source systems that may use different coding schemes.

3. Testing to make sure that the display is correct in a variety of use cases is very important here.

B. Acceptability (+ + +):

1. High, as expected for an intervention that requires no additional user work.

C. Impact (+ +):

1. Moderate to Strong: Expect very high levels of viewing. Where a data display intervention points out a hazard (e.g., a high drug level), impact can be strong. Impact is more moderate for interventions that try to reduce ordering costs [2, 3, 4] (i.e., on the order of 5%–15% reductions in overall charges for the target items[5]).

2. Strong impact as an organizer of all relevant data needed for a given scenario (e.g., a display of completed and due immunizations).

D. Special considerations:

1. Incorrect, missing, or superfluous data can be displayed if underlying codes change (such as if the laboratory changes the method for a given test and assigns it a new code).

2. Test to make sure that the system handles it gracefully if data is requested but the source system for the data is unavailable.

3. Displaying cost data for medications can be challenging. For example, some medications are less expensive at the pill level, but may require a longer treatment course, which may result in overall higher costs.

4. Displaying costs for tests can be problematic because the costs may be different depending on the patient's health plan, and because test costs themselves are often hard to determine; often charges are used as a rough substitute.

E. Examples and subtypes:

1. Health maintenance (disease management) flowsheets:

a) Excellent for at-a-glance display of needed health maintenance tests and therapies specific to a patient.

b) Key element of long-term chronic disease management programs.

c) Immunization charts for children.

2. Test results relevant to an order being entered:

a) Quick way to focus attention on potential hazards suggested by the data.

Key: + (poor), + + (average), + + + (good)

Figure 3-4 *continued*

b) Include drug levels, allergies and sensitivities, key indicators of potential adverse events.

c) Not limited to medication ordering (for example, display of recent hematocrit and status of blood crossmatch [whether an active type-and-screen exists] when ordering a blood transfusion).

3. Displays of potential cost for an ordered or entered item.

4. Displays of justified evaluation and management (E&M) score based on entered data.

5. Population-based reporting:

a) Great way to present data on populations of patients. Important tool to spot practice trends, perform control-chart analysis, and fulfill practice-wide pay for performance criteria.

III. Order Creation Facilitators

A. Ease of development:

1. Order sets: (+ + +) content is Easy if copying from an existing paper order form. Building new order sets, whether for computer or for paper use, is Easy for the first 80% of the work but the last refinements can be Difficult if the order set is to be widely applicable. Keeping order sets current with evolving literature can be difficult.

2. Development of order sets can be done by two major methods:

a) Running a mock order session (entering orders in sequence, just as if one were doing it for an individual patient) is fast and easy to understand, but leaves little room for varying parameters.

b) Tools that create order sets (templates) by placing individual orders on a form make for slower development, but the orders can be better organized and presented, and parameters (such as dose) can be varied through the use of drop-down list controls or text boxes.

B. Acceptability:

1. (+ + +) High, if the right set is easy to find and use. When this is true, order sets greatly increase speed and efficiency. Order sets account for 30–40% of all orders in typical CPOE systems. Highly specific or rarely used order sets may be less acceptable simply because users may not remember that they exist.

C. Impact (+ + +):

1. Strong, since they directly specify the orders that are submitted.

D. Special considerations:

1. As with documentation forms, personal order sets are highly controversial. They clearly improve efficiency, clinician buy-in and convenience and are highly acceptable, but are seen in more and more places as safety hazards.

2. Remember that this concept applies to ambulatory care as well as inpatient care. Order sets (used at the end of an office visit, or to place initial condition-specific orders in emergency medicine) can be powerful tools to improve consistency and optimal care in a rushed environment.

Key: + (poor), + + (average), + + + (good)

Figure 3-4 *continued*

3. It is frequently suggested that order sets lead to excess ordering because the user can easily checkmark a whole string of orders. Empirically, there is probably some truth to this, but detailed studies have not been frequent in the literature.

4. When an order set is used and approved, dozens of orders are submitted in rapid succession. Other forms of CDS must be carefully constructed to handle the possibility of conflicting orders within the set, and to efficiently perform checking and standard reactive alerts on individual orders within the set.

E. Examples and subtypes:

1. Admission order sets.

2. Ambulatory care order sets and templates.

3. Ambulatory care algorithms (e.g., long-term management of hyperlipidemia).

4. Small sets for specific situations (e.g., chest pain protocol).

5. Transfer-postop-preadmission sets: these are order sets that are entered now, but are to be acted upon only after a specific event has passed. These are particularly difficult to implement and require considerable testing because of the possible variations and delays in transfer of care.

6. Multi-person spreadsheets: an unusual form of order set that facilitates ordering of a very specific order type on multiple patients (e.g., patient-controlled analgesia for an entire service, or warfarin orders for an entire unit of post-op joint-replacement patients).[6]

IV. Time-based checking and protocol/pathway support

A. Ease of development:

1. Difficult (+). Requires considerable clinical discussion about what the proper management pathway actually is, followed by significant work to present complex pathways in usable form.

4. Displaying costs for tests can be problematic because the costs may be different depending on the patient's health plan, and because test costs themselves are often hard to determine; often charges are used as a rough substitute.

E. Examples and subtypes:

1. Health maintenance (disease management) flowsheets:

a) Excellent for at-a-glance display of needed health maintenance tests and therapies specific to a patient.

b) Key element of long-term chronic disease management programs.

c) Immunization charts for children.

2. Test results relevant to an order being entered:

a) Quick way to focus attention on potential hazards suggested by the data.

Key: + (poor), + + (average), + + + (good)

Figure 3-4 *continued*

2. Careful scenario testing should be done to ensure the temporal relationship of the various orders in a pathway.

3. Deciding when you need to use a clinical pathway and when you can settle for an order set is the biggest consideration here. Order sets are typically much simpler to build and set up, but pathways may be more appropriate, especially for multi-day, protocol-based care.

B. Acceptability:

1. Medium (+ +). Because these significantly affect the overall plan of care, there can be resistance from end-user clinicians. If the pathway tool is difficult to use, or if patients fall off the pathway too easily, acceptability is likely to be low.

2. For persons dedicated to the pathway or protocol, these tools can be very acceptable and seen as the only way to get clinician adherence.

3. Time-based checks presented as discrete steps (such as alerts or order sets to guide a single step or single day of the protocol) may be easier to use and more acceptable.

C. Impact: Strong (+ + +)

1. When used and accepted, particularly for cancer-treatment protocols, these tools provide a great deal of rigor and prescriptive management—and thus have a high impact on adherence to the protocol.

D. Subtypes:

1. Chemotherapy protocols, often presented as an order set.

2. Admission (inpatient) clinical pathways.

3. Long-term ambulatory care algorithms, usually presented as serial reminders and flowsheet notifications, but based on an overlying long-term algorithm.

V. Reference Material

A. Ease of development:

1. Easy (+ + +) if content comes from well-established, well-structured, well-maintained sources; potentially more difficult to develop and maintain large collections of material locally.

2. Moderate to Difficult to choose the best, most focused reference for a given situation. Highly dependent on the available content sources and their structure. Reference content databases that can be easily segmented (perhaps by using XML or other structuring tools) have an advantage here.

3. Implementation Issues: Reference information can be embedded in virtually all of the other intervention types. It can be linked to an alert, order set or clinical pathway and displayed on ordering forms and various other screens throughout your information systems. As noted in the reference for item 5.2 in Figure 2-5, the emergence of the HL7 infobutton standard is making it much easier to deliver context-sensitive reference information within CIS.

Key: + (poor), + + (average), + + + (good)

Figure 3-4 *continued*

B. Acceptability:

1. Requested reference—High (+ + +)

2. Pop-up automatic reference - Medium to High, (+ +) depending on the intrusiveness of the reference display.

C. Impact: (+ +)

1. Weak to Moderate—relatively low because it does not immediately translate into action. However, impact is higher when the reference display gives specific information necessary for the current management decision.

D. Subtypes:

1. Source:

   a) Commercial reference bases—deserve separate mention because they are often highly structured, segmented, and well maintained.

   b) Locally developed content—often in the form of articles and short monographs.

2. Delivery:

   a) By user request on a distinct reference page or form.

   b) As an available button providing specific information about the clinical item being documented, viewed, or entered (infobutton, KnowledgeLink).

   c) Automatically delivered (e.g., patient's medication schedule produced and printed as part of the discharge process).

3. Clinical Calculators.

E. Special considerations:

1. Try wherever possible to include references and supporting information in other interventions such as alerts and order sets. This can enhance the acceptability and impact of what might otherwise be a weaker intervention.

2. The optimal form of a Reactive Alert always includes some reference material for justification and to help guide the user in considering the proper response to the alert.

VI. Reactive Alerts and Reminders

A. Ease of development:

1. Easy to Moderate for simple alerts (+ +) (responding to one piece of new data, combined with no more than two pieces of existing data—such as a drug allergy alert). Highly dependent on the tools provided for the purpose by the CIS application.

2. As with other types of CDS, specifying an alert with sufficient specificity and sensitivity can be difficult.

3. Moderate effort needed to ensure that the alert is presented in such a way that the user can confidently take action (see CDS Intervention Parameters, page 67).

Key: + (poor), + + (average), + + + (good)

Figure 3-4 *continued*

4. Addressing these challenges often requires that the information system contains and can easily manipulate a wide variety of discrete and nuanced data.

B. Acceptability: (+ +)

1. Highly dependent on the specificity of the alert (the proportion of times that a change in management is truly indicated when the alert appears). However, impact is dependent on sensitivity (the proportion of times that an alert appears when a change in management is indicated) as well—see Impact, below.

2. Cumulative effect of many alerts **("alert fatigue")** can lead to Low acceptability. Reactive Alert capability should be used prudently.

3. Drug-drug interactions based on commercial databases are particularly susceptible to this problem: They can have Low acceptability if the database is configured to show all possible interactions. Most commercial drug-drug interaction products allow users to block presentation of alerts meeting specific criteria (e.g., low severity).

4. Highly dependent on the alert being well-vetted before implementation.

C. Impact:

1. Moderate to High: (+ + +) Alerts are overridden more than 50% of the time in some studies.[7] However, this may be appropriate to achieve necessary sensitivity and to allow for the clinician user to add judgment that a computer cannot easily handle, some reduction in specificity may be necessary.

2. Alert fatigue effect: Impact for individual alerts is higher if alerts fire only infrequently and only for serious conditions.

3. Impact is higher for alerts that correct errors or offer basic alternatives without changing the fundamental plan of care.

D. Examples and subtypes:

Even more than in the above areas, there are many types of reactive alerts. A few specific types are listed here because they have special considerations for selection:

1. Alternative order suggestions—relatively easy to build and to use, these can have High impact if the content warrants.

2. Table-based alerts (drug-allergy, drug-drug interaction).

3. Alerts from abnormal lab or test results—these are often initiated when the user is not actively working on the computer. Thus, these alerts need to notify the relevant user, e.g., by setting off that user's pager.

4. Documentation need—prompt for additional documentation to complete an order, a form, or (more commonly) an encounter.

5. Consequent orders—orders that should be suggested as natural follow-ons to an order just given, e.g., suggested orders for acetaminophen and diphenhydramine whenever a blood product is ordered.

Key: + (poor), + + (average), + + + (good)

Figure 3-4 *continued*

E. Special considerations:

1. Locally-developed alerts should be carefully vetted before implementation and reviewed at periodic intervals.

2. Require at least 0.5 FTE pharmacist to maintain the local versions of the drug information database (drug-drug, drug-allergy and drug-condition alerts).

3. A general rule about alerts is that alerting for true error conditions is often more accepted than alerting for "advice." Be careful to make the advice universally applicable and very well directed at the condition of interest.

4. Testing and content validation is critical because the compliance rate with this intervention may be high.

Key: + (poor), + + (average), + + + (good)

Besides guiding selection of specific CDS interventions to meet specific needs, these figures are also intended as a framework for driving and analyzing research on the pros, cons, and effectiveness of different types of CDS interventions in a variety of circumstances. Some studies are beginning to explore the relative value of different types of CDS interventions,[8] but more such studies are needed.

Benefits Planning Revisited

As you begin thinking in detail about new approaches for improving patient care with knowledge interventions, it is critical to keep in mind the specific (and often quantified) benefits you are trying to accomplish as outlined in Worksheet(s) 1-2. This has been referred to as "designing for benefits" and involves making achievement of the desired objectives an explicit criterion in intervention design.[9] **Use case scenarios** are useful tools for linking design with outcomes in this way.

Use Case Scenarios

Use case scenarios are step-by-step written descriptions of how users interact with a system and the results of these interactions. For example, if an alert is chosen as the preferred intervention to reduce a specific error of commission, use case scenarios can help make explicit how the alert is expected to occur in workflow, what the range of responses is likely to be, and whether or not these responses will help achieve the desired objective.

Use case scenarios for an intervention should cover several different examples of likely user-system interactions and can be divided into a Low, Medium, and High complexity progression. This hierarchy can help isolate areas where the intervention might perform well or poorly based on a specific design approach, which can then be modified if needed.

Use cases should be reviewed with all pertinent stakeholder groups to ensure a shared understanding about the intervention purpose and mechanics. This review can help uncover incorrect assumptions about how the interventions will work or what they will accomplish. Getting this input early in the development process can make it much easier to address any problematic issues that arise. Keep in mind that as intervention development unfolds, you might need to build on the framework of stakeholders you established in Chapter 1 to ensure that all pertinent parties are included in reviewing the use cases.

Use cases developed for design will underpin testing and validation of the corresponding interventions as discussed in subsequent chapters. Often changes to the use cases will occur as review and input broadens, but this evolution can be handled through formal processes for managing the changes.

Measuring Benefits

Intertwined with intervention design and use case scenarios are approaches to measuring the extent to which anticipated benefits are realized. Worksheet 1-2 lays out baseline performance and desired outcomes for target objectives. The sources for data that will document this improvement should be considered during intervention design. Though much of this data ideally should be generated automatically by the information systems that deliver the interventions, these systems often might not be able to do this exactly as desired. Early attention to these measurement issues can help ensure the most practical and efficient path to the needed information, or prompt development of alternative measurement strategies.

Some institutions assign accountability to various positions for achieving target objectives, including using the targets in job performance criteria and in departmental budgets. Though not widely used yet, this can provide powerful incentives for success if implemented properly.[9] As will be discussed in subsequent chapters, this accountability further heightens importance of carefully developing and validating the interventions and assessing their benefits.

WORKSHEET

Selecting CDS interventions that have the greatest chance of enhancing care to achieve your organization's target goals is one of the central tasks of this book and of the CDS programs it is designed to support. You should have a clear understanding of the terms and issues raised in the discussion section of this chapter before completing these worksheets. Keep in mind also that completion of the steps

below is not an overnight process. As with the worksheets in the preceding chapters, it will take careful research, discussion, and deliberation to process and document the required information.

Step 1: Assign an objective class to each clinical objective for which you are developing a CDS intervention.

Step 2: Use the objective classes to help identify optimal CDS interventions and workflow opportunities addressing each corresponding objective, given the capabilities of your available clinical information systems.

CONCLUDING COMMENTS

At this point, you have accomplished the central task of identifying CDS interventions and workflow steps to address your clinical goals and objectives. Selecting CDS interventions is currently more art than science. There is scant research comparing different types of interventions or indicating when each should be used. The information in the figures (e.g., classes of objectives, CDS intervention types, workflow steps) will very likely be refined and expanded over time based on growing global experience with these concepts. The authors would greatly appreciate having readers share insights that they glean from selecting CDS interventions to accomplish objectives. This input will be very helpful in making this guidance in this chapter increasingly practical and useful.

Because the CDS market is at a relatively early stage of evolution, you may find that the functionality you want is not available from your current vendors, or perhaps it is not available at all. A clearer and more unified articulation of information system and content needs for optimally effective CDS could help drive the industry toward providing more robust CDS tools that would better address clinical objectives.

Worksheet 3-1:

Selecting interventions and workflow opportunities to address clinical objectives (through objective classes)

Copy into the first column of this worksheet each objective from Worksheet(s) 1-2 for which you now will be developing CDS interventions. If you are addressing more than one high-level clinical goal, you can use one or more versions of this worksheet.

Use the second column to assign an objective class from Figure 3-1 to each clinical objective in the first column. Keep in mind that Figure 3-1 is a work in progress; this assignment is intended as an aid for selecting interventions; it is not a hard science.

Carry over the desired action from the second column of Worksheet 1-2 to the third column of this worksheet to help with intervention selection.

Use Figure 3-3 as a guide for generating a list of promising CDS interventions and workflow steps for addressing each objective/objective class. Consider the capabilities of your CIS infrastructure, as documented in Worksheet 2-1. Filter these intervention candidates with the selection considerations outlined in Figure 3-4. Document the refined list of targeted workflow steps in the fourth column and the CDS interventions (with the corresponding application following in parentheses) in the fifth column. The final list should reflect a balance between using multiple interventions to increase the likelihood of achieving an objective and not overloading the care delivery system or participants with excessive interventions.

In the sixth column, assign a name to each intervention that can be used as shorthand notation to identify it, for example in subsequent worksheets.

Clinical Objective	Objective Class	Desired Action	Workflow Step	Specific CDS Intervention (Application)	Intervention Name
1. Improve post-op heparin prophylaxis	Prevent errors of omission	Entry of physician order for SC heparin	Ordering	Order set (CPOE)	Heparin in post-op orders
		Nursing check that the heparin has actually been given	Administration	Nursing documentation form (EMR)	Post-op heparin item on nursing documentation form
2. Improve appropriate monitoring of PTT in patients on heparin	Prevent errors of omission	Entry of physician order for PTT	Ordering	Consequent order (CPOE)	PTT consequent order for heparin

Worksheet 3-1 *continued*

Clinical Objective	Objective Class	Desired Action	Workflow Step	Specific CDS Intervention (Application)	Intervention Name
3. Improve compliance with care guideline for enoxaparin	Improve compliance with simple care guidelines	Entry of enoxaparin order in DVT patients without PE	Ordering	Order set (CPOE)	DVT order set
			Ordering	Reactive alert	Enoxaparin alert

References

1 See Table 4: Mapping of order categories in evaluation tool for Leapfrog CPOE standard to clinical decision support, page 16 in www.fcg.com/research/serve-research.asp?rid=41, for an example of how the Leapfrog Group performed a similar mapping in the more limited domain of CPOE.

2 Tierney WM, McDonald CJ, Martin DK, Hui SL, Rogers MP. Computerized display of past test results: effect on outpatient testing. *Ann Intern Med.* 1987;107:569–574.

3 Fischer MA, Solomon DH, Teich JM, Avorn J. Conversion from intravenous to oral medications: assessment of a computerized intervention for hospitalized patients. *Arch Intern Med.* 2003; 163(21):2585–9.

4 Tierney WM, Miller ME, McDonald CJ. The effect on test ordering of informing physicians of the charges for outpatient diagnostic tests. *N Engl J Med.* 1990;322:1499–1504.

5 Bates DW, Kuperman GJ, Jha A, et al. Does the computerized display of charges affect inpatient ancillary test utilization? *Arch Intern Med.* 1997;157:2501–2508.

6 Teich JM, Spurr CD, Schmiz JL, O'Connell EM, Thomas D. Enhancement of clinician workflow using computer order entry. *JAMIA.* 1995; 2(Suppl):459–463.

7 Hsieh TC, Kuperman GJ, Jaggi T, et al. Characteristics and consequences of drug allergy alert overrides in a computerized physician order entry system. *JAMIA.* 2004 ;11(6):482–91.

8 Dexter PR, Perkins SM, et al. Inpatient computer-based standing orders vs physician reminders to increase influenza and pneumococcal vaccination rates: a randomized trial. *JAMA.* 2004;292:2366–2371.

9 Thompson DI, Henry S, Lockwood L, Anderson B, Atkinson S. Benefits planning for advanced clinical information systems implementation at Allina Hospitals and Clinic. *JHIM.* 2005;19(1):54–62.

Additional Web Reading and Resources

- Addressing medication errors in hospitals: 10 tools (Categorization of medication errors: potential technological solutions). http://www.chcf.org/topics/view.cfm?itemID=12682. See various useful worksheets and tables, such as those under Tool No. 5: A guide to potential IT solutions to medication errors.

- Computerized physician order entry: a look at the marketplace and getting started. FCG; December 2001. www.fcg.com/research/serve-research.asp?rid=41. See chapter 3, Introduction to CPOE clinical decision support, pages 12–16.

- How to use an article evaluating the clinical impact of a computer-based clinical decision support system. *JAMA.* http://www.ucl.ac.uk/kmc/publications/pdfs/JAMA1999.pdf.

- Overview of the Leapfrog Group evaluation tool for computerized physician order entry, FCG; December 2001. www.fcg.com/research/serve-research.asp?rid=40. See Table 1, Description of order categories in the Leapfrog CPOE evaluation, page 6.

Chapter 4

Specifying and Validating the Details, and Building the Interventions

Once the set of desirable interventions for achieving priority objectives has been determined, the next steps are to fully specify the intervention details, ensure that stakeholders validate or approve the specifications, and then develop the interventions.

TASKS

1. Define the parameters and logistical details for each chosen intervention to optimize stakeholder acceptance, ease and cost of implementation, effect on workflow, and magnitude of benefit. Document these specifications (Worksheet 4-1, page 79).

2. Validate the proposed CDS interventions with appropriate stakeholders and obtain necessary approvals (Worksheet 4-2, page 82).

3. Develop the planned CDS interventions. Build in technological and people-based mechanisms for gathering and processing feedback from intervention recipients.

Key Lessons

- There are many logistical details about an intervention that need to be carefully established to ensure that it leads to the desired benefit. The nuances of who will receive the intervention and exactly how it fits into their clinical workflow are among the keys to success.

- Feedback on these details from stakeholders, including recipients and others affected by the intervention, should be sought and adjustments made as needed. Those accountable for the interventions and their effects should be comfortable with the plan and its likelihood of success.

- As the interventions are validated and built, make sure that required organizational processes or structural changes are put into place.

- Putting in place a robust plan for gathering and responding to feedback from those receiving or affected by the interventions will help ensure that the rich dialogue with stakeholders that was cultivated during the development stages continues after launch.

DISCUSSION
Intervention Parameters and Details

In Chapter 3 you defined many of the basic parameters for the proposed interventions, including (at a general level) what information will be delivered to whom, as well as where and how in the workflow it will be delivered. Because workflow and CIS tend to be quite complex, there are generally finer details that must be determined before you can develop and launch the selected interventions. This includes specifying more detail about parameters that can affect intervention usability and effectiveness, such as intervention triggers, presentation, recipients, and the like.

Because CDS interventions are tightly coupled with clinical workflow, a central goal of intervention development is to ensure successful integration into this workflow. In some cases, this involves adapting the intervention to the workflow, in other cases, the reverse. In either situation, the nuances of this interaction need to be reflected in the intervention specification.

Below are questions that can help specify intervention details. Although they apply generally to CDS interventions, different intervention types (e.g., alerts compared with templates or reference information) may each have unique logistical issues to consider.

- *When and how is the intervention triggered?* That is, at which exact workflow point in Figure 3-2, page 45, are the interventions triggered? Some interventions are initiated by the information system, while users initiate others. **System-initiated** interventions include those triggered by new data (a specific type of order is entered; a particular event, such as an admission, occurs; a lab result becomes available), or by the passage of time (every night at midnight or eight hours after another event occurs). **User-initiated** interventions include information delivered in response to a user request, for example, for reference informa-

tion about a specific drug or clinical problem, or for a particular order set or flowsheet.

- *What criteria* are evaluated for system-initiated interventions to determine whether specific information is presented to someone after the intervention is triggered? For example, in the case of drug-drug interactions, the interaction-checking intervention is triggered every time a new medication is ordered. The results are delivered to a user only if certain criteria are met; for example, the presence of a severe drug interaction. Triggering and notification criteria for system-initiated interventions must be carefully established to avoid excessive alerting.

- *Where will the patient data come* from that are required by the intervention logic? For example, reminding clinicians when diabetic patients are overdue for a foot examination requires a reliable mechanism for determining when the last foot examination was performed. This determination can be difficult if the information is not recorded and readily accessible to the intervention logic as a coded data element.

- *What exact information will be delivered* to cause the desired outcome? Particularly for system-initiated interventions, such as alerts, what actions can the clinician take in response to the information delivered? In the case of a drug-drug interaction, the intervention might allow the clinician to cancel the current order or to change one of the interacting medications.

- *How is the information delivered?*[1] Several key questions must be addressed. For example, is there a user screen in some application that is updated so that when the screen is accessed the intervention will be apparent? Where on the screen is the intervention presented, and how does that fit into the intended user's workflow and the overall user-friendliness of the screen? Will a system user see a pop-up screen that he or she must address before proceeding? Is an e-mail message or a page sent to someone? To what extent is the intervention output customized to the clinical workflow stage, the clinician, and the patient?

- ***Who will receive the information*** generated by the intervention? This might be a person in a role pertinent to the patient or setting, such as a physician, nurse, pharmacist, or the patient. Where will the recipient be when they receive the intervention (e.g., the bedside or exam room, at the patient's home, or in the pharmacy, nursing station or clinical office)? What, if any, HIPAA data privacy and security implications[2] must be considered regarding transmission and storage of patient specific data?
- ***What are the feedback channels*** whereby intervention recipients can communicate concerns and input about intervention usability and value? This feedback is critical for solidifying intervention adoption and building trust in the overall CDS program.

Optimizing Intervention Specifications

The answers to the questions above for each of your planned interventions will provide many of the details for your intervention specifications. Below are some recommendations that will help you ensure that these specifications lead to optimally effective, safe, and usable interventions.

Optimizing Effectiveness

- ***Provide clear and practical recommendations*** in any intervention that offers advice to the user.
- ***Link advice to action opportunities*** as much as possible to optimize translation of the information into the desired action. This can be accomplished through techniques such as including the ability to initiate recommended orders with a single mouse click or keystroke

directly upon receiving the advice, as in an alert.

- ***Link interventions to each other when appropriate.*** Consider other opportunities to join interventions (from Figure 2-5, page 33) in a manner that will increase their effect. Besides linking orders or order sets to alerts, documentation templates or reference material also can be linked to order sets to facilitate appropriate documentation or learning along with the alerting function. By increasing the delivery of more knowledge into fewer workflow steps, other intervention combinations can similarly provide enhanced value compared to implementing them independently.
- ***Consider the cascade of events*** that the intervention is designed to initiate and ensure that the organization is prepared for these events. For example, when an intervention is designed to increase use of underutilized screening tests such as mammograms or clinical interventions such as flu shots, the volume of tests or interventions may rise significantly. Preparing affected units for intervention success with adequate capacity and supplies will help ensure that the CDS intervention achieves its overall intended result.
- ***Consider communication factors for interventions directed to patients.*** These factors include the patient's native language, level of formal education, culture and ways of receiving information, such as the presence of a telephone or Internet access in the home, and personal beliefs about health and illness. These can play a critical role in whether or not the desired messages are effectively communicated.

Optimizing Safety

- ***Consider unintended negative consequences*** that the intervention might have on the process and outcomes of care.[3, 4, 5] There is increasing attention to these potential adverse information technology effects, but sensitivity and attention to these issues early during design should reduce the chances for problems after launch.

- *Develop a fail-safe* plan in case the CIS underlying the CDS interventions become temporarily unavailable. Reasons for unavailability may include scheduled system maintenance or an unanticipated malfunction. Anticipate and attempt to mitigate any implications for patient safety from such events.
- *Minimize intervention overload,* especially with alerts. While individual interventions might be quite valuable, overloading users with more information than they can handle can actually increase distractions and decrease safety.

Optimizing Acceptability and Use

- *Ensure that intended recipients can access and act on the information* with the greatest ease and least disruption possible. This requires careful planning and extensive user input on exactly how the information will be presented and used in workflow. Maximizing the value of the information while minimizing the effort to access and apply it will optimize the intervention use and usefulness.[6]
- *Provide evidence and rationales* supporting any clinical recommendations. This supportive information should be readily accessible but should not slow the reader in digesting the key recommendation and proceeding with patient care activities. Although clinicians might not necessarily interrupt patient care workflow to read the material, they value knowing it is there because it helps establish confidence in the recommendations and provides a source for further research, if desired.[7]
- *Provide appropriate customization* and tailoring of the intervention, when possible, related to the setting, specialty, workflow context, practice case-mix, provider, patient-specific factors, and so on. The extent to

which individual users should be able to configure some specific interventions is controversial. For example, while users generally prefer maximum flexibility, many organizations do not permit individuals to customize order sets (which would reduce the ability of this intervention to minimize practice variations and can present substantial maintenance problems).

- *Provide incentives* wherever possible for effective use of CDS interventions. Because the interventions may often interrupt normal workflow, it will be helpful to consider approaches to minimize their disruptive effect and optimize value. As discussed in Chapter 1, pay-for-performance programs may represent a powerful driver for CDS use, though it is important to consider whether or not the user of a particular intervention is receiving the incentive.

    In addition, providing continuing medical education (CME) credits, when appropriate, for using CDS content can provide another incentive for clinicians to take the time to review it. In early 2005 the American Medical Association (AMA) approved a policy for providing AMA Physician's Recognition Award (PRA) Category 1 credit (a type of credit on which U.S. requirements for physician CME are typically based) for physician directed, interactive Internet-based CME.[8] This includes researching answers to clinical questions and documenting their application to practice via reference-type CDS interventions.

Special Considerations for Alerts

Alerts will be an important component of many CDS programs because they can significantly affect care decisions. However, because of their intrusive nature, careful attention to how they are managed and delivered is essential. Below are additional issues to consider in establishing detailed specifications for alerts.

- *When* is the most opportune time to deliver the alert? Do not underestimate the annoyance caused when a clinician's thought process or interaction with the patient is interrupted by an out-of-context alert. In practice, alerts are often dismissed.[9] While some of this is a result of improper thresholds for delivering an alert, experience suggests that intrusive alerts, even important ones, may be ignored if delivered at an inopportune moment.

- *Who* will get the message (including when and how) if an unsolicited alert is delivered during a time when the intended target is not available to receive it? This is known as **alert escalation**. For example, how will a clinician covering for another clinician who is the intended alert recipient access the system area where the alert is delivered? How will this escalation protocol be established and maintained?

- *How long* will an intervention be available to the recipient if it is stored in a patient's electronic record? Will it be presented to only a specifically named recipient, only one member of a class of recipients, or to every member of the class? For example, when issuing an alert regarding a patient's potentially life-threatening hypokalemia (low blood potassium), you may want to notify everyone that accesses the patient's electronic record. Less urgent interventions may be presented only to the patient's primary care clinician. The question of whether a log of access to the intervention (i.e., who saw which intervention and that individual's response to the intervention) is maintained is a potentially controversial one with uncertain implications for malpractice liability (see Appendix B, page 117).

- *How urgent* is the intervention, considering the rapidity of deleterious effects on the patient if an action recommended in an intervention does not occur? In light of the urgency, is it necessary for the recipient to acknowledge that the communication has

been received? If so, what is the maximum delay before a lack of acknowledgement prompts escalation of the intervention? Does the alert stop workflow until it is addressed? Can it be overridden, and, if so, is a reason required?

- *Which medium* will be used to convey the message (e-mail inbox, wireless and/or handheld device, pager, EMR/CPOE screen, printed encounter sheet or turn-around document)?[10] For example, an intervention that is being offered to improve patient compliance with screening tests (such as a reminder issued to a woman to schedule an appointment for a screening pelvic examination) may be delivered by a less urgent mechanism (e.g., postal letter) than one that involves potential harm to patients (warning about laboratory test results that may indicate life-threatening conditions) that might be delivered in real time via pager to a clinician.

- What is the expected average and maximum number of *alerts per patient* and clinician? Excessive alerting is an important factor in negative perceptions of individual alerts and to the alerting component of the CDS program. You can prioritize alerts by the importance of the objective they are intended to address (see Figure 1-8, page 10), and focus alerts initially on the most promising targets. Pioneering organizations in CDS that have large numbers of alerts in the system use various schemes to limit alert exposure. In Chapter 6, page 99, and Appendix D, page 121, we discuss techniques for assessing **alert burden**. The discussion in Chapter 3 provides a framework for appropriate use of alerting. We will return to this important issue in the coming pages.

- *Will unwanted interactions* among alerts occur because of their number and nature? The testing steps discussed in the next chapter can help detect this problem, but ideally it should be considered and prevented as new alerts are specified.

- What is the proper **notification threshold** to maintain adequate sensitivity yet minimize negative workflow effects (such as causing nuisance alerts or requiring more time or effort to accomplish a clinical task)?[11]

- Is it appropriate and technically feasible to allow recipients to **opt out** of specific alerts in general or for a specific patient (for example, to indicate to the system, "don't show me this again...")? Should recipients be allowed to alter the notification parameters? Under what circumstances, if any, should patients be able to modify alerts or opt out of receiving them?

- When and how can previously issued alerts be **retracted?** In some instances, the data used to generate an alert may be discovered to be incorrect after the intervention has been received. In these situations, you must devise a mechanism for issuing a correction or retraction of the intervention.[12]

- How are alerts **dismissed or overridden?** In some cases (e.g., for alerts with particularly high clinical stakes) it may be desirable to require the user to enter a reason if the alert recommendation is not followed. Consider building into such alerts a standard list of override reasons in a menu, with an option to explain or add additional reasons in free text. These standard override reasons might include items such as: MD disagrees with recommendation, recommendation already implemented, alert fired inappropriately, patient ineligible for recommended intervention, patient refuses recommended intervention, and the like. Studies have examined allergy alert overrides and made specific recommendations for improving these alerts.[13]

Use Cases and Organizational Issues

The use case scenarios you began developing in Chapter 3 can be revisited now in light of the many additional facets that the above considerations brought to light. The use cases can help you visualize how these issues will affect user interaction with the intervention, which can in turn be used to help refine the use cases if needed. It will be important to ensure that the use cases are in synch with the final specifications, as they will be used later in validating the intervention after it is built.

As you work through design specifications for the interventions themselves, do not forget about the workflow process, and cultural and organizational issues that are intertwined with the content and mechanics of the interventions. For example, new organizational structures might be needed for tasks such as developing or approving content for new CDS interventions and creating new workflows required for their successful uptake. Developing effective feedback channels for the CDS interventions might also require cultural or organizational changes, especially if robust mechanisms for this type of CIS user feedback are not already in place.

These process and organizational factors related to interventions will be key to realizing expected benefits. Any needed changes should be addressed explicitly in specification development and documentation. Doing so can help ensure that any obstacles or special needs are identified and addressed early.

Involving Stakeholders

The investments made to identify stakeholders and cultivate champions early in your CDS efforts can pay off at this stage. Those who will be affected in some way by the CDS interventions are in a great position to help filter all the considerations discussed so far in this chapter into the intervention specifications. Remember to consider stakeholders who are both respected opinion leaders and those with formal leadership positions, those whose jobs will be affected by the intervention, and those workers who capture data necessary for the intervention.

Those who will actually build the intervention are also key stakeholders at this stage. Their feedback on whether the proposed details can be developed within the time and resource constraints will be critical input for moving forward. Overall, broad input into the intervention specification can lead to a more effective end product due to improved system design, neutralized objections, and a greater sense of ownership among all stakeholders.

Pay careful attention to resistors and detractors as their concerns[14] can be a vital source of information about deployment issues that might interfere with the intervention success. Detractors generally come into play for interventions that tend to disrupt workflow or engrained practice patterns. Their concerns might include liability fears (see Appendix B: Medico-legal Considerations with CDS, page 117), alert fatigue, user interface complexity, extra time requirements, and reduced clinician autonomy. Making potential detractors a part of the team that is developing and validating the CDS interventions may convert them to champions, and former skeptics can be the best salespeople for the interventions. Regardless of how the detractors are addressed, however, care should be taken to treat them with respect. While it is easy to dismiss detractors of CDS interventions with proven clinical benefit as hopelessly out-of-date and overly conservative, marginalizing detractors in this way may only harden their opposition and create major problems during and after launch.

In the case of some detractors, even the most energetic efforts to solicit their opinions and accommodate their objections will not lessen their opposition. In such a situation, transparency is key and includes broad representation among the stakeholders and an open development process. Benefits and limitations of the intervention design should be discussed freely. This can help neutralize potential objections from detractors about the development processes. Some objections might be that the CDS program represents the wishes of a few individuals, or that decision support knowledge established as effective elsewhere lacks sufficient customization to be effective locally.

Maintaining broad representation and a transparent process for specification development can help ensure that any remaining detractors are seen as not reflecting the organization's overall commitment to the intervention. Communication is key here. Advertising campaigns and informational messages (such as e-mail notes, mailed brochures, and departmental meetings) can be used to provide frequent updates about program development and to acknowledge disposition of prior objections and concerns about the program. Such communication can give the entire organization a sense of ownership of the emerging intervention.

Validating the Specifications

After addressing the above considerations in your intervention specifications, you are ready to validate the plan with stakeholders. The discussion about stakeholders in Chapter 1, page 1, provides the backdrop for intervention validation. Figures 1-1 through 1-3 should help you identify the key individuals, positions, and committees that should participate, and appropriate roles for each. Hopefully you have involved many or all of these stakeholders in the planning and design stages, but at this point, more formal sign-off on the specifications can occur. For example, key stakeholders who will build, deploy, evaluate, support, and use the interventions should have the opportunity to review (if not formally sign off on) the specifications.

Accountability for CDS Results and Their Measurement

Important questions to keep in mind at this validation stage include, Who is responsible for measuring the CDS results? Who is accountable for these results? A picture of the responsible parties for your individual and collective CDS interventions begins to emerge from your organization's version of the CDS roles and responsibility as shown in Figures 1-2 and 1-3. This picture may include many staff and leadership stakeholders from different clinical and service departments who are responsible for various aspects of CDS implementation and evaluation. It is important to clarify exactly where in this matrix overall responsibility lies for achieving the specific benefits that the CDS interventions are designed to achieve (i.e., as will be outlined in Worksheet 4-1, page 79).

Departmental operations leaders may assume responsibility for documenting and delivering benefits from individual CDS interventions that seem to fall within their purview. However, these leaders are generally not in an optimal position to identify benefits that accrue across departments as a result of improved communication or better process integration. An organization-wide benefits realization team made up of individuals with a broad array of pertinent expertise can be a much more powerful approach. The team ideally should possess expertise in clinical, technical, administrative, financial and medical informatics-related health services research areas and should report to a group of key executives. Such a team was mentioned in Chapter 1. If you have not considered forming one yet, you might want to consider doing so in conjunction with your intervention validation rounds.

This team has the potential to develop, articulate, and communicate a clear vision of the benefits that are expected from the various clinical decision support interventions. Additionally, the designation of a new interdepartmental team should improve coordination of the overall benefits realization process and reduce the likelihood that individual departments will fight over credit for specific benefits that have been achieved. Finally, by allowing this new team to focus time, energy, and attention on the problem of identifying and documenting various benefits, the final result should be a more standard, higher quality, credible, and defensible report.

The responsible parties should directly oversee the implementation of the various system features and work process changes necessary to achieve the benefit goals. Some experts on benefits realization advocate including such accountability for the target results in individual job-related performance goals

and/or in pertinent departmental budgets. When this is the case, it is clearly essential that those responsible for the CDS outcomes formally sign off that the proposed interventions are appropriate for realizing the intended benefits. Any major concerns should be addressed before further development of the interventions.

Efforts to quantify the benefits of CDS interventions require significant financial and human resources in their own right, not to mention the resource requirements for developing and implementing the interventions themselves. Because careful and ongoing measurement is a key part of any continuous improvement process (of which CDS programs are certainly an example), this investment is essential.

Even with the best intentions, plans, and execution, the CDS evaluation methods and results can be subject to intense scrutiny and criticism by stakeholders, especially when budgets and/or compensation are tied to the results. A collaborative relationship among stakeholders, fostered by leadership and governance structures, can help ensure that the evaluation process and outcomes meet the organization's needs. While all of the expected benefits may not be achieved at the expected levels, a thoughtful and explicit approach to planning for and realizing benefits can still yield more positive results than if benefits realization is left to chance.

Building the Interventions and Feedback Mechanisms
Content, Mechanics, and Organizational Issues

Creating intervention content and mechanics based on the design specifications usually requires some combination of writing computer programming code, configuring parameters in installed CIS, developing new CDS content, and integrating external CDS knowledge sources (see Figure 3-4). For most organizations, time and expertise limitations will make extensive programming impractical. Developing substantial amounts of new CDS content internally will be similarly impractical for many organizations, though it is critical to provide some degree of internal review and approval for all CDS content that is deployed. In many cases then, intervention development will consist primarily of utilizing CDS features provided by your CIS and CDS vendors and adding/customizing/reviewing content as needed (e.g., for documentation forms, order sets, alerts).

The careful attention to workflow processes and cultural and organizational issues paid during the earlier steps should be carried forward through the build step. Continue putting in place any needed environmental components needed to ensure intervention success.

Feedback Mechanisms

In addition to developing systems that deliver the interventions to recipients, it is important to build feedback mechanisms for assessing the use and response to the interventions, particularly unsolicited ones such as alerts. This includes mechanisms that enable recipients to provide feedback about specific interventions, ideally in a convenient manner soon after their interaction with the intervention.

For example, if a recipient believes that a particular alert is inappropriate or some other piece of delivered information is inadequate in content or presentation, there should be one or more channels associated with the intervention (or perhaps the underlying information system) to communicate any concerns to an appropriate person. It should be clear to users exactly when and how they are able to provide feedback, and the channels should be adequate for handling the types and quantity of expected input. Similarly, there should be mechanisms to gather implicit feedback about interventions (for example, an intended recipient is failing to respond to an alert).

Other desirable feedback mechanism features include:

- Prompt implementation team responses (e.g., one to two business days), with at least an

acknowledgement, and ideally with an indication of whether the user can immediately solve their own issue or whether a change in the system is called for. Quick responses on the part of application developers and the implementation team to user identified bugs or incomplete design considerations works wonders by letting users know that their voices are being heard and that their input is valued.

- Clearly informing users as to when they can expect to see their suggestions incorporated into the application, if a change is needed. By clearly communicating a phased plan for handling bugs and modifications to existing intervention specifics, an unprioritized and inefficient "put-out-the fires" approach can be avoided.

Feedback mechanisms should include those that originate from the project team (e.g., formal/informal surveys, observations of intervention use) as well from the users (e.g., via e-mail links, helpdesk phone numbers). Proactively seeking and encouraging this feedback (and responding to it) can lead to much less overall aggravation than if the frustrated user has to come looking for the implementation team.

Ideally, both manual and technological channels for gathering feedback about intervention function and use will be developed. These can include:

- Direct observations of users (clinicians/patients) interacting with the system in live or test environments;[15]
- Subjective user feedback (both spontaneously submitted and periodically solicited);
- Input from clinical champions (and patient champions for interventions provided directly to this group); and
- Objective measurements of intervention usage (e.g. provided by the CIS delivering the intervention).

Processes should be put in place to periodically and systematically gather and evaluate feedback from these channels. Key issues to consider in the evaluation include:

- How often is each intervention used (e.g., reference material accessed, specific order sets and templates completed)?
- How often are alerts presented? Heeded? Overridden?
- What do users perceive as the intervention's effects on workflow? Their perceptions can include whether interventions are delivered at an appropriate point, message content is considered appropriate and useful, response time is acceptable, and performance and access are reliable.

Chapter 6 will explore in depth how to process user feedback and apply it to improving the interventions. When you are developing the feedback mechanisms, keep in mind that the more CDS intervention recipients believe that the implementers are responsive to their needs and concerns, the better partners they will be in achieving the desired outcomes.

Project Management

Formal project planning and management can be helpful for even simple interventions (e.g., links to reference materials). However, it is essential for interventions with any complexity and/or significant workflow impact (e.g., complex protocols or alerts). Specific roles, responsibilities, and timelines should be agreed to by the project team and documented.

Ideally, a project manager skilled in such assignments will assume responsibility for shepherding the intervention through validation and development as outlined in this chapter. That same role should also guide the interventions through testing and launch as outlined in Chapter 5 and evaluation and refinement as outlined in Chapter 6. Whether or not there is a designated project manager, the roles and processes outlined in Figures 1-2 and 1-3 will need to be managed. Do not hesitate to involve the stakeholders mentioned in these figures in helping to address any questions or challenges that arise during the build phase.

WORKSHEETS

Step 1: Define and document the parameters and logistical details for each chosen intervention to optimize stakeholder acceptance, ease and cost of implementation, effect on workflow, and magnitude of benefit. Document these specifications.

The completed Worksheet 3-1, page 67, contains a list of CDS interventions that you intend to develop and deploy to achieve specific target objectives. Before you build the interventions, you must develop specifications for the detailed behavior of the intervention. This includes not only the content and mechanics of the intervention, but also the associated feedback channels and workflow and organizational changes necessary to ensure intervention success in meeting objectives.

Think carefully about how each planned intervention will affect workflow, including that of clinicians, support staff, patients, and others. The interventions almost inevitably will require alterations in typical routines. The goal is to have targeted individuals perceive the changes as positive to the greatest extent possible. Identify ways to ensure that information is delivered in a format and at a time that will be most conducive to its being acted upon appropriately. Answering the questions and addressing the issues in the discussion section of this chapter can help you with these specifications.

Worksheet 4-1 can be used to document your specifications. The completed form is used in two primary ways at this stage: to obtain validation and approval by key stakeholders in the proposed plan and then to guide those who will be responsible for building the interventions. Although all specification elements are potentially relevant to both audiences, each might be most interested in a somewhat different set of elements. The information in these forms will also come into play during launch and evaluation, discussed in the next two chapters.

The collection of these completed intervention specification forms documents the portfolio of planned/launched interventions within your organization's CDS program. It reflects the high level CDS

Worksheet 4-1:

Intervention specification form

A separate specification form should be completed for each intervention you plan to build. In the example below, the specifications most pertinent for validation and development have been divided into separate worksheets that illustrate with different interventions how the form might look for these two purposes. Depending on your style, the needs of your organization, and the nature of the specific intervention, you can either combine these two forms for each intervention or keep them as separate forms.

The first several rows of the validation version carry over data from Worksheet 3-1 (i.e., intervention name, clinical objective, desired action). This provides context for reviewers.

Baseline performance and desired outcomes for the interventions are drawn from Worksheet 1-2. The performance improvement targets may have evolved in the vetting process up to this point, but now is the time when key stakeholders will sign off on delivering against these targets. It might not be practical to assign hard quantitative targets for every single intervention. Nonetheless, the more aggressive you are about defining and cultivating measurable benefits, the more likely you are to reap tangible and meaningful improvements from your efforts.

More than one intervention might be focused on achieving the target. These interdependencies can be noted in item 5 in the worksheet.

The remaining items on this validation form reflect the various specifications that result from your dialogue, analysis, and vetting of the issues and questions earlier in this chapter. The items on the developer's specification form that follows also come from these explorations.

Specification form for validation[16]
Intervention Name: Flu shot (influenza vaccination) reminder system

1. **Clinical objective:** Increase the number of eligible patients who get flu shots in our outpatient practices.

2. **Desired action:** Identify eligible patients who have visits each day; put reminders to give flu shots on the standard printed schedule sheet.

3. **Baseline performance:** Currently less than half of all high-risk patients are receiving flu shots. In addition, less than 20% of the general population receives flu shots.

4. **Desired outcome:** Reduction in outpatient visits related to the flu and hospitalizations of high-risk patients.

5. **Associated interventions focused on objective:** Radio and television ads reminding high-risk patients to get flu shots; postcard reminders sent to all high-risk patients.

6. **Workflow step:** Printing and distribution of daily schedules with reminders attached, pre-visit check-in for patients.

7. **Specific CDS Intervention and pertinent CIS application(s):** Use the scheduling application along with clinical data warehouse to identify patients eligible for flu shot reminders; import list of eligible patients into application responsible for printing daily schedules.

8. **Approach:** Determine eligible patients who have visits today; put reminders to give flu shots on the standard printed schedule sheet.

Worksheet 4-1 *continued*

9. **Clinical background:** Flu shots should be offered to eligible patients. In the past, mailings to patients have not been effective at increasing flu shot use. Many patients have not received flu shots even though they had a regular visit with their provider.

10. **Selection criteria:** Use CDC guidelines to determine which patients are eligible for flu shots and the duration of season in which to offer them.

11. **Exclusion criteria:** Patients whose health record data shows a flu shot for the current flu season, or who have an egg allergy.

12. **Target population for intervention:** Primary care physicians and nurses in outpatient practices.

13. **User interface:** Printed suggestion to offer flu shot, if appropriate, at bottom of schedule sheet.

14. **Monitoring:** Assess whether patients who meet eligibility criteria get printed reminders; monitor proportion of patients getting flu shots.

15. **Evaluation:** Analyze proportion of eligible patients in practice who receive flu shots.

16. **Primary stakeholders:** Directors of ambulatory practices.

17. **Clinical champion for this project:** Dr. Phyllis Smith.

18. **Urgency/required delivery time:** Before September 1.

19. **Whose jobs do you expect to be affected by this project?** Practice managers or secretaries who print schedules; providers; nurses or assistants who administer flu shots.

20. **What are possible adverse consequences of implementing this project?** What if the reminder is given on a patient who had a flu shot already (elsewhere, or here but after reminder was queued or printed)? Will implement mechanisms to prevent extra flu shots.

Specification form for developers

CDS intervention name	Heparin in post-op orders
Description:	When post-op order sets are displayed, an item to order heparin (for thrombosis prophylaxis) will always be included
CIS application affected	CPOE
Intervention type	Order set modification
Workflow step	Ordering (at post-op time)
Specifically triggered by	All post-op order sets except: patients already on heparin, enoxaparin, warfarin
Presentation type	Order set item
What (information presented)	Order heparin 5000 units subcutaneously twice a day
Alerting	None
Who (user)	Ordering clinician
Action items	Checkbox allows user to order heparin
Feedback channels and plan	Contact information for responsible department already exists on order set

and clinical goals addressed by the program, and the corresponding clinical objectives that the interventions are designed to address.

Step 2: Validate the proposed CDS interventions with appropriate stakeholders and obtain necessary approvals.

Hopefully you will have had extensive input from and dialogue with all pertinent stakeholders at each step so far in this book (e.g., in defining objectives and mapping out interventions and their details). Now is the time to confirm that the interventions you have specified are ready (and approved) to be built. Figures 1-2 and 1-3, pages 4 and 5, respectively, provide a framework for the roles and interactions pertinent to this validation and approval process. If you have not done so already, it might be useful to create a version of these figures now to reflect the specific CDS-related roles and their interplay in your organization. It will come in handy for the remaining tasks in this book as well.

In this round of interactions, you will be ensuring that your proposed CDS interventions, both individually and collectively, are acceptable to key stakeholders and recipients, fit into workflow, are likely to achieve their desired outcome, and will not adversely affect other healthcare processes. In some organizations and circumstances (e.g., high-stakes interventions), it might be useful to document formal sign-off to proceed by appropriate leadership.

Step 3: Develop the planned CDS interventions. Build in technological and people-based mechanisms for gathering and processing feedback from intervention recipients.

Careful attention to specifying and validating the CDS intervention plan should pay off when it comes time to create the CDS interventions. For example, developers should benefit from the clear and detailed direction in Worksheet 4-1 on exactly what is to be built and what objectives the product is expected to achieve. Similarly, the investment in cataloging the available CIS infrastructure and selecting and designing interventions with those capabilities in mind should help minimize any surprises for developers.

The oversight group will help resolve inevitable issues that arise during development, ensuring that the intentions and objectives previously defined for the CDS intervention are factored into the compromises and modifications that creep in. When this happens, the specifications in Worksheets 4-1 should be updated so that they continue to accurately reflect the intervention details.

Building the feedback channels may include a combination of work on the intervention itself (e.g., adding "contact us" information or buttons on display screens) and on organizational processes (e.g., ensuring that a knowledgeable person can be easily reached in a timely manner by users to address concerns about the intervention). If any changes to the feedback plan or channels arise in the course of development, make sure these too are reflected on Worksheet 4-1.

CONCLUDING COMMENTS

The tasks outlined in this chapter depend heavily on the work accomplished in the preceding chapters. Ideally, clear articulation of CDS program goals, objectives and interventions derived from broad-based and iterative input will simplify intervention development. Similarly, this shared vision supports the workflow redesign that will accompany these interventions, and that will help determine the success or failure of the CDS interventions. Continuing this people-oriented project approach with the tasks here should similarly set the stage for a successful program launch in the next section.

Remember that your organization does not have an unlimited capacity to absorb the changes required to develop and implement CDS interventions. As a result, you should carefully consider the time frame and order in which interventions are implemented.

After this stage in the process, you will have developed your next round of CDS interventions and you will have a clear picture of their anticipated costs and benefits. Although the next section discusses rollout planning in detail, it is worth reassessing now whether all of your planned interventions

Worksheet 4-2:
Specification validation and approval form

This form documents your discussions with various stakeholders about the completed intervention specification forms. If you have a relatively small number of objectives and interventions you are validating, you can put them all on one form; otherwise it might be better to have a separate form for each objective or even each intervention.

You can use this form to document all your validation discussions with the many different stakeholders to help keep track of the various comments, or use it only to document final sign-off by the approvers. Similarly, you can record discussions and comments from individuals, committees or both. The CDS program notebook that we recommended you create in Chapter 1 can be particularly useful in this step.

Clinical Objective	Intervention Name	Reviewer (Role)	Date Presented	Comments	Date Approved
Improve post-op heparin prophylaxis	Heparin post-op order set	Jim J. (Chief resident [graduate medical trainee] in surgery)	3 Jan 2005	Need to make text clear that neurosurgical patients should not receive this therapy	5 Jan 2005
Improve PTT monitoring in heparin patients	PTT Alert	Mary K. (Nurse manager, PCAU)	3 Jan 2005	Need to educate nurses on the prophylaxis policy so that they will comply with the alert; approval withheld pending training plan	
	PTT Order Set	Jim L. (Surgery)	3 Jan 2005	None	5 Jan 2005
Improve compliance with care guideline for heparin and low molecular weight heparin	Heparin guideline reference link	George D. (Division chief of cardiology)	3 Jan 2005	Need to clarify that link will fire for both inpatient and outpatient locations	5 Jan 2005

can be successfully handled by your organization in the next implementation round. If resources are tightly constrained, consider starting small by first launching interventions that have a high benefit-to-cost ratio, documenting effects and building on early successes.

References

1 Kuperman GJ, Teich JM, Tanasijevic MJ, et al. Improving response to critical laboratory results with automation: results of a randomized controlled trial. *JAMIA*. 1999; 6(6):512–22.

2 Centers for Medicare and Medicaid Services. HIPAA-Administrative Simplification. http://www.cms.hhs.gov/hipaa/hipaa2/default.asp.

3 Ash, JS, Berg M, Coiera E. Some unintended consequences of information technology in health care: the nature of patient care information system-related errors. *JAMIA*. 2004;11:104–112. DOI.

4 Ihealthbeat, 12/21/04: http://ihealthbeat.org/index.cfm?Action=dspItem&itemID=108108.

5 Koppel R, Metlay JP, Cohen A, et al. Role of computerized physician order entry systems in facilitating medication errors. *JAMA*. 2005; 293:1197–1203.

6 http://www.healthsystem.virginia.edu/internet/familymed/docs/info_mastery.cfm. See equation for usefulness of medical information under "What is information mastery?"

7 Ely JW, Osheroff JA, Chambliss ML, Ebell MH, Rosenbaum ME. Answering physicians' clinical questions: obstacles and potential solutions. *JAMIA*. 2005;12:217–224.

8 Internet Point of Care Policy in the CME section of AMA's Web site: www.ama-assn.org.

9 Weingart SN, et al. Physicians' decisions to override computerized drug alerts in primary care. *Arch Intern Med*. 2003;163:2625–2631.

10 Kuperman GJ, Teich JM, Bates DW, et al. Detecting alerts, notifying the physician, and offering action items: a comprehensive alerting system. *JAMIA*. 1996;3(suppl):704–70.

11 See Krall/Sittig references in additional Web readings and resources section for systematic analysis of usability and usefulness requirements for alerts and reminders.

12 Kuperman GJ, Hiltz FL, Teich JM. Advanced alerting features: displaying new relevant data and retracting alerts. *AMIA Proceedings*. 1997:243–7.

13 Hsieh TC, et al. Characteristics and consequences of drug allergy alert overrides in a computerized physician order entry system. *JAMIA*. 2004;11(6):482–91.

14 Ash JS, Stavri PZ, Dykstra R, Fournier L. Implementing computerized physician order entry: the importance of special people. *Int J Med Inform*. 2003;69(2-3):235–50.

15 Nielsen J. *Usability Engineering*. San Francisco: Morgan Kaufmann; 1994.

16 Adapted from Abookire SA, Teich JM, Bates DW. An institution-based process to ensure clinical software quality. *AMIA Proceedings*. 1999; (1-2):461–5.

Additional Web Reading and Resources

CDS implementation recommendations distilled from one institution's extensive experience:

• Bates DW, Kuperman GJ, Wang S et al. Ten commandments for effective clinical decision support: making the practice of evidence-based medicine a reality. *JAMIA*. 2003;10:523–530.

Research documenting usability and usefulness requirements for computer-based clinical alerts and reminders:

• Krall MA, Sittig DF. Clinicians' assessments of outpatient electronic medical record alert and reminder usability and usefulness requirements. *AMIA Proceedings*. 2002;400–405.

• Krall MA, Sittig DF. Subjective assessment of usefulness and appropriate presentation mode of alerts and reminders in the outpatient setting. *AMIA Proceedings*. 2001;334–338.

Work regarding system architecture required to implement decision support interventions:

• Jenders RA, Hripcsak G, Sideli RV, et al. Medical decision support: experience with implementing the Arden Syntax at the Columbia-Presbyterian Medical Center. *AMIA Proceedings*.1995;169–173.

• Hripcsak G, Clayton PD, Jenders RA, Cimino JJ, Johnson SB. Design of a clinical event monitor. *Computers and Biomedical Research*. 1996;29(3):194–221.

Chapter 5

Putting Interventions into Action

After specific CDS interventions are developed, the next step is to ensure that they perform as expected in the test and production environments and then to introduce them carefully into the patient care process.

TASKS

1. Before launch, test the CDS intervention content, mechanics, and logistics (Worksheet 5-1, page 93).
2. Develop and implement an intervention rollout plan that addresses user communications, training and feedback, as well as responsibility for monitoring implementation status (Worksheets 5-2 and 5-3, pages 94 and 95, respectively).
3. Gather, document and address user feedback before, during, and after intervention rollout (Worksheet 5-4, page 96).

Key Lessons

- Careful and complete testing of all new CDS functionality, along with other CDS and CIS systems that might be affected, is essential to ensure that the completed interventions perform as expected. The details of this testing depend on the type of CDS intervention, the nature of the clinical content, and the underlying technology used to create the CDS intervention.

- Make sure that everyone who will use, or might be affected by, the new CDS functionality is well informed about project status and upcoming events to minimize surprises and optimize their constructive participation.

- Anticipate users' training needs and provide training opportunities that fulfill them as conveniently as possible for the users.

- Consider the nature of both the CDS intervention and the clinical and technical environment when determining the speed, scope (which clinical units) and order (which interventions or units go first) for rolling out new CDS interventions.

DISCUSSION

The goal of this stage is to ensure that the interventions you specified in Chapter 3 and developed in Chapter 4 will be disseminated successfully to intended recipients and achieve the desired results smoothly and efficiently. As noted previously, successful interventions will have a significant effect on clinical decision making and workflow, so carefully managing this change is critical.

Clearly, the processes and workflow routines that CDS interventions alter are complex. They may involve many different individuals and roles, be stressful, have high stakes, and be multifaceted. It is essential to understand the current processes in detail, as well as the effects that the new interventions will have. Careful planning, testing, and rollout are required to ensure that intended recipients embrace the decision support and use it effectively. The collaborative approach outlined in the previous chapters should provide a solid foundation for success at this stage.

As with previous steps, your version of stakeholder/management in Figures 1-2 and 1-3, pages 4 and 5, respectively, will determine who will be responsible for and oversee CDS intervention launch. Depending on the breadth and complexity of interventions to be launched and your organizational resources, there may be several individuals or teams responsible for the different testing, communication, and support tasks at this stage.

CDS Intervention Testing

The details of your testing approach will vary somewhat depending on the type of CDS intervention, the nature of the content, and the underlying technology of the CDS intervention. For example, simple links to reference material on an Intranet site would not require as much testing as a new patient-specific alert. If you have modified or expanded the CDS functionality in an existing clinical information system (e.g., how rules are handled), then you need to test both the new functionality and any underlying functions that might have been modified

or affected. On the other hand, if the CDS interventions only involve adding specific rules or other content to an existing and well-functioning CDS application, then testing can focus primarily on the new components.

The basic steps in a standard **quality assurance** (QA) approach are outlined below. They can be adapted as needed to address the specific needs of your implementation. There are a variety of resources available with additional details on QA procedures[1] if you need more information on this topic.

Use Cases and Testing Scenarios

The use cases that you developed in Chapter 3 and refined and validated in Chapter 4 are now used to test your completed interventions. If significant time elapses between when the scenarios were vetted and this testing stage, you should ensure that they remain valid and appropriate according to clinical users and experts, including those who were not necessarily involved in their development. All validated use cases should be included in the final software requirements documentation.

Typically, one or two basic use cases will be developed that relate to the intervention's primary objective. For example, the use case for a drug-allergy alert might consist of a drug order for a patient with a documented allergy to the drug. With further thought, many special cases and unusual situations can be envisioned (e.g., drug is ordered from a drug family that is cross-allergenic to the patient's documented allergy; drug is ordered to which patient is allergic but alert has been overridden in the past; person viewing the alert is not authorized to make a final decision on whether or not it is safe to give the drug). The basic use cases should derive from business needs. The others result from taking a hard look at the basic case in light of rich clinical knowledge and practice experience. Stakeholders can provide helpful input here. Use case variants are an important way to catch needed design changes before launch.

If you did not already do it as part of the tasks discussed in Chapter 4, you can now develop the narrative use cases into formal **testing scenarios**. These scenarios describe exactly how the user will interact with the intervention and the results of that interaction. Any changes necessitated by testing and made to either the scenarios or the system design should be reflected in the corresponding documentation. These testing scenarios will be used both by developers and end-users in the testing steps outlined below.

Unit Testing

Software developers perform this testing to ensure that the application will deliver the CDS intervention as it has been built and that it functions as designed, independent of other parts of the CIS. It involves applying the testing scenarios to ensure that valid inputs produce valid and appropriate outputs. Various invalid inputs that might occur in practice should also be tested to ensure that they are handled appropriately.

For technically straightforward interventions, such as links to reference material or documentation templates, this testing will be relatively simple. For more complex interventions, such as alerts that process a lot of patient-specific data, all logical branches and internal program flow should be validated. **Unit testing** for these more complex applications may involve the use of special software for debugging and testing. This testing is typically the responsibility of the application developers, not the software QA staff. If staffing levels permit, developers not directly involved in creating the component should do unit testing.

Integration Testing

Once all of the individual intervention components are working as designed, the next step is integration or **functional testing**. Here, system developers and administrative staff ensure that all of the individually developed system components work as designed (e.g., as called for in the use cases) when integrated

with the existing CIS infrastructure. For example, **integration testing** verifies that the CIS response time is adequate at both peak and steady-state use levels after the new interventions have been added. **Regression (verification) testing** might also be necessary when the new intervention involves significant modification to the underlying CIS. This selective testing ensures that all new software is working as expected *and* that no new bugs have been introduced that could result in the failure of previously working functions.

User Acceptance Testing

This final pre-launch testing is performed by clinical end-users to ensure that the system works for users as intended and meets all of the planned business and clinical requirements. This testing often begins with the testing scenarios that have been developed from the use cases. After the system has been shown to handle these successfully, users can be asked to go through several "real-life" situations or scenarios of their own. The selection of the end-users to perform this testing is critical to ensure that the results accurately reflect the broader user experience with the intervention after launch. Representatives of all the pertinent user groups should be included, as emphasized in discussions about working with stakeholders earlier in this book.

If you have not done so already, test the user feedback channels. Make sure that e-mail links, calls to help desk and pager numbers, and the like are routed and responded to appropriately.

Beta Testing/Pilot Launch

After the intervention has successfully passed all of the testing phases above, it is ready to be moved to the live CIS and patient care environment. When a new intervention does not disrupt workflow very much and is not controversial (e.g., straightforward links to reference material), it is often appropriate to release the intervention to all clinical users at the same time. For very complex or intrusive interventions (e.g., multi-step protocols or workflow-interrupting alerts), it can be helpful to release the intervention initially to a few selected clinical users, such as a single practice or inpatient unit.

During this pilot or **beta testing** period, an easy and convenient method for providing feedback to the intervention deployment and development teams is particularly important. You should make sure you have adequate staff to seek out and respond to this input to help ensure success during the subsequent full-scale rollout.

Full-live Evaluation

Once the intervention has proven successful during limited use, it is ready to be released to the full population of intended users. The feedback channels will serve as the means whereby the implementation team can assess user response to the system. We will discuss ongoing evaluation in greater detail in Chapter 6.

Not all CDS interventions will require an extensive testing procedure. Nonetheless, a thoughtful testing approach can help prevent surprises from derailing the positive results expected from CDS program planning and intervention development. It can also help engender confidence in the program and individual interventions from both leadership and end-users.

Launch Communications

Users and others who will be affected by CDS interventions about to be launched should be well informed about forthcoming rollout events to minimize surprises and optimize their constructive participation. During the pre-launch phase, gaining widespread CDS recipient buy-in on the interventions (particularly unsolicited ones such as alerts) and their delivery details can help ensure that these individuals will handle delivered materials appropriately after launch. Communications about the launch set the tone for this acceptance.

It can be helpful to frame these implementation details with the broader goals, strategies and vision for the CDS program. Sharing (and getting feedback

on) this context can help the organization "see the big picture," which can help drive appreciation and adoption of near-term tactics embodied in the forthcoming interventions. It can also help pave the way for more successful development and launch of subsequent interventions as the CDS program unfolds.

If you have followed the approach outlined in the preceding chapters, there will already have been extensive communications with many different stakeholders about the new CDS intervention(s), and broader goals and strategies, well before launch. Selected stakeholders will have helped identify the need and objectives, develop the intervention specification to optimize benefits and minimize workflow disruption, and test the finished product. Historically, lack of sufficient communication during these early stages has been one of the most common causes of problematic and failed CIS and CDS implementations.[2, 3]

Even if key stakeholders have been involved throughout the process, there will usually be many users who have not been as deeply connected to the unfolding details. They too will need to be brought up to speed on the why, what, and how of the intervention (in addition to the broader CDS program context) so that they respond in a manner that helps achieve the desired outcomes. Sharing details of how stakeholder input was gathered and used in earlier stages can help reassure these users that their needs were carefully considered during design and development. Be sure to also consider how support staff and others who are not direct recipients will be affected by the interventions, and how best to educate and engage them in the process.

Launch-related communications should be two-way. Just as in earlier interactions with stakeholders, it is important not only to convey the CDS goals, strategies and tactics, but also to listen for concerns and opportunities to improve the approach. Not every issue raised will necessarily be addressable in the current implementation round. Nonetheless, if the broad community of users knows that their concerns and suggestions are sought and taken seriously, it can help build their trust in the CDS program and implementation staff.

As discussed in Chapter 1, champions can play a crucial role in communicating with the user community about new CDS interventions. These individuals can include early technology adopters, clinical thought leaders, clinicians closely connected with management, "**super users**" who quickly learn new systems and are happy to share their knowledge with others, and some who have combinations of these characteristics. Ideally, intervention champions will broadly understand the value and importance of clinical decision support, convey this message to their colleagues, and model successful intervention use after deployment. Champions can also share specific examples from their experience of how interventions have been useful and effective, which can help spur adoption.

Ideally, clinical proponents of an intervention who are thought leaders should be an initial source of communication to all other affected users before launch. This can help avoid strong negative reactions that can occur when a clinician suddenly feels that "the computer has changed the plan" without prior warning.

Be creative and think broadly about opportunities and forums to get the word out about the new CDS intervention(s). Both informal exchanges and more formal presentations should be considered. For example, clinical staff meetings (e.g., held by doctors, nurses, pharmacists) and department meetings around launch time can be opportune times for thought leaders and champions to present the intervention to their colleagues and gather feedback. Workflow problems or other negative intervention side effects that have been missed in the design phase can often be caught here. It is important that the proponents be well informed about the interventions so they convey accurate information. They should also keep an open mind to constructive input and not to be defensive about "protecting" the intervention.

Other channels to let users know about the launch of new CDS interventions include formal advertising campaigns, e-mail notices or printed brochures, bulletin boards, and the like. These may have been set up earlier in the process for major new initiatives, as outlined in Chapter 4. If not, they can be utilized now during launch, as appropriate.

Since the CDS interventions and program will evolve over time, maintaining and using effective communication channels is an ongoing process. As with the earlier project phases, it is essential to be alert for any generalized negative response to intervention components and for individual detractors. These problems are not likely to go away after launch unless they are addressed thoughtfully and directly. A collaborative approach to moving forward with the CDS plan based on recognition of shared goals (e.g., optimizing the process and outcomes of patient care), stakeholder needs and organizational constraints is generally the best tack for these potentially difficult situations. You can review the "Involving Stakeholders" section in Chapter 4, page 74, for more specific tips on identifying and dealing with detractors.

As noted in Chapter 4, potential liability issues surrounding how alerts are handled are a source of concern for some stakeholders (especially physicians who are targeted to receive clinical alerts). Organizations are encouraged to consult with counsel on potential liability issues. We are not aware of any directly pertinent case law, and believe that it is possible to implement alerts and other CDS interventions in a manner that minimizes this concern (e.g., by providing mechanisms to document why an alert has been overridden and making it difficult to override absolutely critical alerts). See "special considerations for alerts" in Chapter 4 and Appendix B: Medico-legal Considerations with CDS, page 117, for more information.

Training

Having raised awareness among those targeted by a CDS intervention, the next step is to ensure that these users will interact with the intervention in a manner that leads to the intended benefits.

Normally, formal training is required when new CIS applications are implemented (e.g., CPOE or electronic clinical documentation), but not when relatively straightforward CDS interventions are launched. However, if the intervention represents a significant change in workflow or has a user interface that is not intuitive, explicit training on effectively incorporating it into daily routine may be necessary.

Below are some suggestions about training users on new CDS interventions.

- Investigate **training resources** provided by your CIS and CDS content vendors; they may have training options that can help users understand and effectively use the intervention. Ask about printed materials, web sites and other computer-based offerings, or live training programs.

- Consider a *"train the trainer"* approach (i.e., developing a cadre of people who understand the intervention well and are able to formally teach others about it). This can be very helpful if a large training force is needed (e.g., for a significant new project involving workflow change for a large group of users).

- Make **training documentation** available prior to training sessions, so users have a reference to consult before and after the session.

- **Schedule training conveniently.** The first training group should include key representatives of the various departments that will be affected by the intervention. For full launch, training should be scheduled at multiple, varied times (including "non-business hours," if possible) so that a busy user can find a convenient slot. Remember that computer-based and printed materials can potentially serve as an around-the-clock training resource.

- **Tailor training** duration and intensity to user needs and constraints. In a hospital, for example, nurses may have more formal mechanisms and allocated time for information system training. Physicians often require a more informal and ad hoc process, so shorter, more focused training may be necessary. To avoid degradation of the effect of training, it should be scheduled relatively close to the time the intervention is deployed.

- Pay careful **attention to expressed concerns** and non-verbal communication during this training (especially from those who were not "friends of the project" during earlier stages). This can provide helpful insight into potential difficulties that might arise as the intervention rolls out into practice.

- Remember that **most "training" will occur after launch.** Whether or not there is a formal training program, users will develop skill and comfort with the intervention by using it. It can be extremely helpful to cultivate a cadre of "super users" who understand the intervention well and can provide support and encouragement to their colleagues. You can revisit the section "Working with Implementation Champions" from Chapter 1, page 11, for more guidance on this.

Intervention Rollout

As discussed in Chapter 2, there is an intimate relationship between an organization's unfolding CIS infrastructure and the CDS interventions that depend upon (and help generate value from) that infrastructure. Launching point-of-care clinical information systems such as CPOE and EMRs can be major undertakings that consume substantial organizational resources, time, and attention. In some cases, CDS interventions (e.g., as outlined in Figure 2-5) will be launched at the same time as these systems. The testing, communication and training tasks outlined above for CDS will then need to be incorporated into the corresponding items for the CIS launch.

Since a major CIS launch can be fraught with its own challenges and user-acceptance issues, careful consideration should be given to the costs and benefits of complicating this with anything but the most straightforward CDS interventions. Waiting until the underlying CIS infrastructure is solidly and successfully in place before overlaying potentially problematic CDS interventions is the prudent course in many cases.

The rollout schedule for CDS interventions deserves careful attention even when the pertinent CIS infrastructure is stable. The nature of both the CDS program and the environment should be considered when determining the speed, scope (which clinical units first), and order (which interventions first) for launching an intervention. For example, issues that affect these launch variables include the urgency in addressing the underlying clinical objective, the breadth of the CDS program (whether it is limited in scope or a comprehensive suite of interventions), and the capacity of the implementation team and intervention recipients to absorb new interventions.

While one or a few simple interventions might be rolled out quickly without any problems, more complex or multi-pronged initiatives might require a phased launch. For example, there might be a few interventions developed as part of the CDS program to accomplish each of several different clinical objectives. Some of these interventions might be intrusive. The planning team will need to decide whether to launch these all at once or to use a phased rollout approach. Once again, it is often wiser to use a phased or incremental rollout that allows the intervention itself, and related launch and implementation details, to be iteratively fine-tuned with successively broader audiences.

Similarly, for interventions such as alerts that are potentially disruptive to workflow and counterproductive if not implemented properly, it can be helpful to launch them initially with a small number of users or in selected locations. Such limited **live testing** can uncover problems not previously identified from development testing. This phased release for a potentially problematic intervention provides an opportunity to work out problems that might occur with its routine use, before exposing large numbers of recipients to it.

Factors to consider when choosing pilot launch locations include (1) how representative they are (whether the patients, clinicians, and workflow are typical for those environments where the intervention ultimately will be deployed), (2) size (too many clinicians and patients may prevent a thoughtful appraisal of the testing, while too few may afford inadequate opportunities to test the intervention), and (3) availability of support staff (especially true in geographic locations remote from the main facility or IT department). Additional considerations for selecting pilot sites for CIS and CDS implementations are outlined in Appendix C: Pilot Site Selection, page 119.

The overall goal for the rollout plan is to simultaneously optimize the speed at which benefits are realized and the magnitude of those benefits. This goal is accomplished by disseminating the interventions in the most successful manner that is as painless as possible to all stakeholders. Specific interventions that offer the greatest prospect for returns with the least disruption are logical starting points. Insights are emerging from the literature on CIS implementation that can provide some guidance for CDS rollout.[4]

In considering appropriate sequencing for CDS interventions, keep in mind that some interventions (especially alerts) might more strictly reinforce specific clinical policies already in effect but not well heeded. For example, an intervention might make it impossible to order a restricted medication in a CPOE system without required approval. In instances where the policy might be somewhat unpopular, consider decoupling its enforcement with the corresponding CDS intervention launch. In this case, one approach might be to more strictly enforce the policy by other methods beginning several months before the CDS intervention launch. This can reduce negative reactions to the policy itself, which would complicate the launch of the CDS intervention. Conversely, CDS interventions that reinforce policies that are beneficial to recipients (e.g., interventions aimed at care practices tied to enhanced reimbursement in pay-for-performance programs) can be launched at a time and manner that leverages this support.

It is also wise to have some type of celebration to mark a successful launch. The scale should be appropriate to the importance and difficulty of the intervention(s) rolled out. This may seem unnecessary, but there are significant benefits that can be derived from such a celebration. First, it serves as a milestone event that makes all users aware that this implementation round is essentially "complete," though bug fixes will be ongoing and enhancements may be released in subsequent rounds. It can also be a time to review expected intervention benefits with the user community. Perhaps, most importantly, it can help reinforce the partnership between the implementation teams and the user community on using the CDS program as a helpful tool in achieving key objectives.

WORKSHEETS

Step 1: Before launch, test the CDS intervention content, mechanics and logistics.

Use the testing discussion, above, as background for tailoring a testing strategy appropriate to your organization and the interventions you are launching now. Make sure that use cases still accurately reflect the important business and clinical needs implicit in the clinical objectives, and that the testing scenarios will effectively challenge the interventions with these needs.

Bear in mind that most CIS vendors will test the programming that underlies CDS interventions they support (e.g., rules engines for alerting), but that any local customizations may require additional testing. Similarly, verify that any processing done to incorporate clinical knowledge into the CDS intervention has not changed its clinical meaning or effect.

Be particularly attentive to user testing results; they can help assess widespread user readiness for the interventions and identify the need for additional education, support or incentives to ensure successful adoption. This testing can also uncover difficulties, such as unexpected or counterproductive side effects, workflow implications, or costs associated with the intervention. Potential remedies that can be instituted before launch may emerge from these evaluations. However, the careful analysis and validation steps already accomplished should significantly reduce surprises at this late stage.

Worksheet 5-1 is used to document pre-launch testing for each intervention.

Step 2: Develop and implement an intervention rollout plan that addresses user communications, training, and feedback, as well as responsibility for intervention monitoring.

Review the discussion above on rollout communications and training if necessary, and consider the components that will be most helpful for launching your interventions. Make sure you fully leverage your investment in cultivating champions for these tasks.[5]

Make sure that by the time any interventions are launched, ongoing routines to monitor and support the intervention's content and delivery mechanics are already in place. This will be discussed in greater detail in the next chapter, but the initial plan needs to be developed and put into place at this stage. The plan should include the party responsible for the intervention and an initial monitoring frequency.

Such a maintenance plan is important because both the clinical knowledge base from which CDS interventions are derived and the technology infrastructure through which they are delivered are in a constant state of flux. As a result, some elements of the testing you did prior to launch will need to be repeated in a regular fashion. Maintenance issues will inevitably arise because important new knowledge is available and must be incorporated, or because adding new clinical content or enhancements to underlying clinical information systems changed intervention behavior in undesirable ways.

Use Worksheet 5-2 to document your plan to notify the affected community about the upcoming launch, train them on effectively using the intervention, gather their feedback after implementation, and assign responsibility and timetables for intervention maintenance. This document can be used to build a clear and shared picture about plan details for the

Worksheet 5-1:

Pre-launch testing

Professionals in your information services division or the consulting company that is building your interventions will generally complete this worksheet. It is organized by intervention type, since that is generally how the testing will be conducted. In the second column, list all the interventions you will be launching. You can carry them over from one of the earlier worksheets (e.g., Worksheet 4-1 or 4-2). Organize these interventions by type (i.e., from Figure 2-5, page 33), and list the corresponding type for each grouping in the first column.

In the third column, Test Scenario, outline the range of patients and parameters for which testing should be done. The last three columns are used to document when and by whom the testing was done, the results, and other pertinent notes that the testers wish to convey back to the implementation team.

Intervention Type	Intervention Name	Test Scenario	Date/ Tester	Results	Notes
Alerts	Heparin post-op alert	Enter the order for transfer to PACU into the order entry system for five test patients whose bed status indicates that they are in the OR. Do not enter an order for heparin prophylaxis. Ensure that alert fires and alert text is appropriate.	3 Jan 2005/ John B.	5/5 alert fired correctly	No issue
	PTT alert	Enter an order for transfer from PACU to ward for five patients. Enter an order for IV heparin, but do not enter an order for PTT. Ensure that "asynchronous alert" queues up for nurse to retrieve at next administration time.	3 Jan 2005/ John B.	2/5 correct. Alert only firing for some wards and not others	Re-work and re-test
Order Sets	Heparin post-op order set	Order post-op heparin from the post-op order set on five patients. Ensure that order goes through properly to nursing and that appropriate reference material on the use of the drug is attached.	25 Jan 2005/ Jill A.	5/5 correct	None
	PTT order set	Order heparin from the ordering menu as well as the search engine and ensure the PTT orders are connected to all ways of ordering IV heparin for 10 occurrences.	25 Jan 2005 Jill A.	10/10 correct	None

Worksheet 5-2:

Intervention launch plan

This sample worksheet is organized by the clinical information system through which the CDS intervention is delivered. Depending on the number and types of interventions you are launching at this stage, and how the components of your plan interrelate, you might want to organize it differently (e.g., by clinical objective). Similarly, if there are several major components to your launch, you might want to create a separate worksheet for each component.

For each intervention to be launched, outline the communication and training plan in the third column. In the fourth column, list the post-implementation feedback channels and how you will use them. Remember to include feedback mechanisms that are both user-initiated (e.g., e-mail links within interventions), and implementation team initiated (e.g., surveys and interviews), as appropriate.

The worksheets in Chapter 4 document intervention stakeholders, clinical champions and approvers. The fifth column in Worksheet 5-2 documents the position, committee or department responsible for overseeing the intervention and its performance after launch.

The last column can be used to record additional items that might be pertinent to each of the three plans outlined in this worksheet.

Clinical Information System	Intervention Name	Communication/ Training Plan (pre-implementation)	Feedback Plan (post-implementation)	Intervention Maintenance Plan	Notes
Better Care-CPOE	Post-op heparin alert	E-mails, pizza lunch, internal newsletter, log in screens	Interview with surgical residents scheduled for one week after activation	Quality department will do quarterly report to pharmacy and therapeutics committee	Quality dept. will need reports on post-op heparin orders on a regular basis
	Heparin post-op order set		Same as above	Same as above	
	PTT alert		Review with nurse manager on post-op ward scheduled for one week post activation. He will collect information from his staff.	Nurse quality review committee will review every six months	Nurse quality review committee is just getting started. Need to continue to support.

Worksheet 5-3:

Implementation status

This worksheet is a working document that provides a snapshot of the interventions you are rolling out, individually and collectively. Once again, the set of interventions being rolled out can be organized in a variety of ways; in this sample, by pertinent information system.

Recording the date testing starts in the third column identifies when the intervention enters the rollout sequence of events. It can help alert you to interventions that might be stuck at this stage. The fourth column indicates when this testing is complete and the intervention is potentially ready for launch.

The fifth column indicates the target date for initially launching each intervention. Seeing all these dates together can be helpful for sequencing and appropriately spacing out the individual intervention launches, and making modifications to the schedule as needed. The actual launch dates and locations in the sixth and seventh columns track the progress of your rollout. This can be helpful both for reporting progress to other stakeholders and for tracking the pace at which the organization can deliver and absorb new interventions.

Information System	Intervention Name	Testing Started	Testing Complete	Planned Launch Date	Actual Launch Date	Locations/ Users
Better care-CPOE	Post-op heparin alert	3 Jan 2005	3 Jan 2005		4 Feb 2005	9 North 8 South
	PTT order set	25 Jan 2005	25 Jan 2005		4 Feb 2005	Internal medicine
	PTT alert	3 Jan 2005	19 Jan 2005		4 Feb 2005	

implementation team, and also to gather input from selected stakeholders to help optimize the plan.

A key component of the rollout plan is whether and how interventions will be launched in phases. Worksheet 5-3 is used to track these rollout details. It is especially useful if more than a few interventions will be launched in this cycle, or if individual interventions will be launched in several stages. Besides overall project tracking, it can serve a variety of specific needs, including planning for and allocating personnel for intervention testing, training, and support.

Step 3: Gather, document and address user feedback before, during and after intervention rollout.

Beginning with testing and continuing after launch through ongoing monitoring and maintenance, users will provide feedback that will help you improve intervention acceptance and benefits. Systematically documenting this important input, as well as whether and how it is addressed, is key to optimally benefiting from it. Worksheet 5-4 can be used for this purpose.

Worksheet 5-4:

Feedback issues and resolution

Each intervention you are launching should be listed in this worksheet. In this sample they are organized by underlying information system, but you can use whatever scheme best meets your needs.

Record all of the substantive feedback you receive for each intervention through the various channels in the fourth column, indicating the date and source for the feedback in the third column.

Although the details might not be immediately apparent, a plan for addressing each substantive issue should be documented at some point in the fifth column. When the issue is resolved, that can be noted in this column as well; the sixth column can be used to indicate the target or actual date for resolution, as appropriate. Use the last column to indicate the priority for addressing the issue (e.g., low, medium, or high).

Information System	Intervention Name	Feedback Date and User	Feedback	Plan/ Resolution	Target Date/ Actual Date	Priority
	[General CDS-related comments]	4 March 2005— Juan V.	Overall there are too many false positive alerts related to medication prescribing.	Plan to form workgroup to explore what additional steps can be taken.	First meeting target: May 2005	Medium
Better care-CPOE	Heparin post-op alert	16 March 2005— Victor E.	Alert appears to be firing at appropriate times; residents think it is OK.	None		
	PTT order set	30 March 2005 Jill G., MD	Order set is well received and being used.	None		
	PTT alert (nurses)	3 April 2005 George H., RN	Nurses express extreme dissatisfaction. Doesn't fire at appropriate time in workflow and unclear how to act on it.	Review triggers and try to rework so that it fires only on documentation of heparin.	Review to be completed by mid-April	High
	PTT order set	15 March 2005	Well received, no major issues.	None		

Worksheet 5-4 can be used to help prioritize intervention enhancements into a predictable schedule rather than a shotgun approach to changes. It can also help communicate to users that their input is being heard and taken seriously. Finally, it can be used in discussions with management to help justify resource needs for ongoing system enhancements.

CONCLUDING COMMENTS

This launch phase marks both an end and a beginning. The complex planning and development stages culminate in the actual delivery of knowledge interventions to clinicians and patients. This in turn begins the process of modifying their behavior to measurably improve outcomes.

Once again, this process is more of a change management challenge than a technological one. Success will depend on the extent to which barriers have been anticipated and addressed in the earlier phases. Similarly, a launch that smoothly and effectively addresses communication, training, and rollout phasing creates the foundation that will lead to expected benefits being realized. Creating short-term wins with CDS interventions in areas that are important to key stakeholders will help demonstrate the value of the CDS program, diffuse skepticism, and build momentum.

Even before any CDS intervention delivers knowledge to an end user, it is likely that your organization will have reaped significant benefits from its emerging CDS program. For example, the focus on identifying and prioritizing CDS goals and considering strategies for addressing them will likely have beneficial effects on related process- and outcome-improvement activities beyond the specific interventions now being launched. Hopefully, these CDS interventions themselves will also generate substantial returns, but it is worth considering these related side effects so you can cultivate these additional benefits.

The next step in the performance improvement cycle is ensuring that the launched interventions achieve their desired results and are continually maintained and improved. Chapter 6 explores this challenge in detail.

References

1 See, for example: Galin D. *Software Quality Assurance: From Theory to Implementation.* Boston: Addison-Wesley; 2003.

2 Massaro TA. Introducing physician order entry at a major academic medical center: I. Impact on organizational culture and behavior. *Acad Med.* 1993;68(1):20–5. PMID: 8447887.

3 Dykstra R. Computerized physician order entry and communication: reciprocal impacts. *AMIA Proceedings.* 2002:230–4. PMID: 12463821.

4 Lorenzi NM, Smith JB, Conner SR, Campion TR. The success factor profile(s) for clinical computer innovation. *Medinfo.* 2004;2004:1077–80.

5 Krall MA. Clinician champions and leaders for electronic medical record innovations. *The Permanente Journal.* 2001;5:40–45.

Additional Web Reading and Resources

• Bodenheimer T, Grumbach K. Electronic technology: a spark to revitalize primary care? *JAMA.* 2003;290:259–264. http://jama.ama-assn.org/cgi/content/abstract/290/2/259.

• Doolan DF, Bates DW, James BC. The use of computers for clinical care: a case series of advanced US sites. *JAMA.* 2003;10:94–107. http://www.jamia.org/cgi/content/abstract/10/1/94. See especially the discussion of use of decision support and implementation success factors.

• Metzger J, Fortin J. *Computerized Physician Order Entry in Community Hospitals; Lessons from the Field.* 2003; California HealthCare Foundation and First Consulting Group. www.chcf.org/documents/hospitals/ CPOECommHospCorrected.pdf.

Chapter 6

Measuring Results and Refining the Program

After CDS interventions are launched, their effectiveness in achieving the intended benefits should be monitored on an ongoing basis. Positive and negative effects on workflow and other processes should be evaluated as well. Based on the organization's goals and objectives, the CDS program should be modified as needed to optimize the beneficial effects of the CDS interventions individually and collectively.

TASKS

1. Assess intervention use and usability on an ongoing basis (Worksheet 6-1, page 106).
2. Evaluate intervention performance against objectives (Worksheet 6-2, page 109).
3. Continually enhance the value to users as well as the impact on goals and objectives of individual CDS interventions and the overall CDS program (Worksheet 6-3, page 110).

Key Lessons

- Key stakeholders and organizational leadership can help establish reasonable measurement intervals and expectations for improvement. Evaluating intervention effectiveness requires both quantitative and qualitative approaches.

- **Log files** and other approaches to tracking intervention use can be helpful for monitoring intervention effects. Details of interest include when and how the intervention was invoked, where the user and patient were at the time, when in the workflow it happened, and how the information delivered was handled and applied.

- Plan on iteratively refining interventions to improve their use and benefits. Opportunities will unfold based on lessons learned and data amassed during each implementation round, evolving capabilities in your CIS infrastructure and available CDS tools, new clinical knowledge, and the changing environment in healthcare.

- It is important to have a systematic approach to managing organizational knowledge assets. This includes policies (e.g., covering periodic content review) and infrastructure (e.g., committees and **knowledge management** tools) to ensure that the quality, currency, and appropriateness of all the content in CDS interventions.

DISCUSSION

The effects of CDS interventions must be analyzed carefully to ensure that the considerable resources required for their implementation yield the intended results. This analysis will demonstrate whether interventions are being used as expected (and as appropriate). In addition, it can help quantify return on investment, both financially and clinically. The analysis may require comparing post-intervention data with pre-intervention baselines concerning clinical processes/workflow, satisfaction, specific healthcare outcomes, or other measures.

Evaluation permeates the entire CDS implementation process, reflected by the multiple vetting and evaluation steps in the preceding chapters. As noted previously, because the clinical environment and clinical knowledge base are so dynamic, this analysis must be ongoing. Figure 6-1 demonstrates this graphically and illustrates that subsequent rounds of system enhancement will involve revisiting many of the previous steps in this book. The initial passes should help you create a solid foundation and provide useful tools to facilitate future cycles.

Evaluating Alerts

Although alerts are not appropriate for all CDS needs (as Figures 3-3 and 3-4 illustrate), they can be useful tools and figure prominently in many CDS programs. Because they can also cause substantial problems (e.g., with workflow efficiency and user acceptance),[1] a thoughtful approach to evaluating their use is in order. Some of the issues underlying this analysis also apply to evaluating other intervention types.

Tracking Alert Firing and User Responses

A first step in evaluating alerts (applicable to other interventions too) is to track the details of when and how the alert is invoked or fired. This includes details of what exactly is triggered, where the user and patient are at the time, when it occurs in the workflow, and how the information delivered is handled. Figure 6-2 is an example of a log file that captures this data. IT staff can often generate such a file with support from the vendor for the CIS through which the alerts are delivered.

In the early stages after launching alerts, this log can be very helpful in catching problems with alert appropriateness (e.g., as indicated by a large number of overrides). If left unchecked, this situation can trigger strong negative reaction to the alerts from users.

A "perfect alert" would theoretically always fire when appropriate and provide the user with information they consider useful. Correspondingly, it would never fire at inappropriate times or deliver information that wasn't helpful to the user. Unfortunately, the current state of the art for alerts is far from this ideal for a variety of reasons, including the lack of access by the rule logic to coded clinical data needed to calculate inclusion and exclusion criteria for each alert. Despite your careful attention to considerations discussed in previous chapters for developing good alerts, there will likely be a significant number of rejected alerts in your log. Keep in mind that some users may reject alerts even when they are appropriate; there are a variety of reasons for this, including alert fatigue. Potentially "acceptable" reasons for overriding common types of alerts include:

- **Drug allergy alerts:**[2] Aware/will monitor; patient does not have this allergy/tolerates; patient taking already; other
- **Drug-drug interaction alerts:** will adjust dose; will monitor; patient already tolerated medication; no reasonable alternatives; other

The implementation team can examine alert override reasons for patterns among various clinicians or even entire departments. These patterns can point toward potential strategies for reducing the number of overrides, which may indicate wasted time or goodwill, or missed opportunities to improve care.

There are other alert-related statistics and reports that can provide additional insights into how users are interacting with these interventions and what

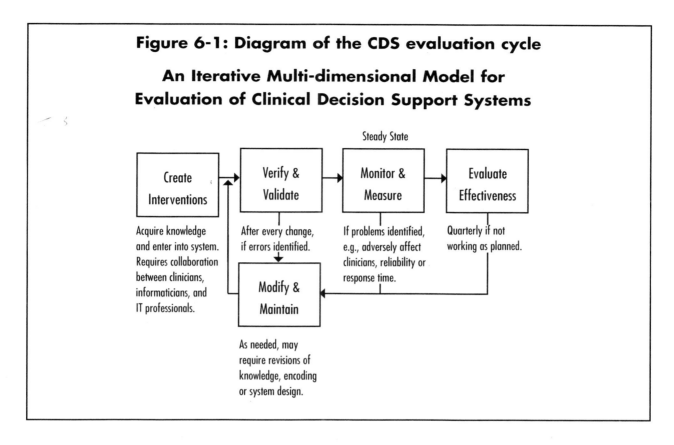

Figure 6-1: Diagram of the CDS evaluation cycle

An Iterative Multi-dimensional Model for Evaluation of Clinical Decision Support Systems

Steady State

Create Interventions → **Verify & Validate** → **Monitor & Measure** → **Evaluate Effectiveness**

Modify & Maintain

Acquire knowledge and enter into system. Requires collaboration between clinicians, informaticians, and IT professionals.

After every change, if errors identified.

If problems identified, e.g., adversely affect clinicians, reliability or response time.

Quarterly if not working as planned.

As needed, may require revisions of knowledge, encoding or system design.

the implications of these patterns might be. Several of these are discussed in Appendix D: Additional Statistics and Reports for Evaluating Alerts, page 121.

The worksheet section of this chapter presents a detailed approach for accomplishing each of the three central tasks above for CDS program monitoring and enhancement. Before turning to the worksheets, we first explore the key maintenance-related issue of CDS knowledge management.

Managing Organizational CDS Knowledge Assets

As we have emphasized throughout this book, fully achieving individual clinical objectives may require delivering multiple CDS interventions to various care participants at different points in workflow. Since CDS programs will often consist of many clinical objectives comprising larger goals, and several different goals, the number of individual CDS interventions deployed in an organization can become large. Ensuring the quality, currency, and appropri-

ateness of this collection of content assets is essential to keep the knowledge interventions safe and consistent with best clinical practices.

Currency and Appropriateness

All CDS interventions need to be re-evaluated regularly to ensure that the clinical knowledge they convey is accurate, up-to-date, and delivered in a way to achieve the desired outcome. Because the technical and content components of the CIS infrastructure can be complex, changes to these components in one part of the information system may require repeated testing to ensure that other inter-related parts of the system continue to behave as expected after the change.

Similarly, because the evidence base and expert opinion on which best practices rest are continually shifting, it is essential to ensure that the content underlying the CDS interventions remains synchronized with this knowledge. Some organizations assign responsibility for the different content areas to

Figure 6-2: Alert log file

Alert	Provider ID	Patient ID	Physical Location	Date/ Time	Alert accepted, rejected or simply closed.	Override reason
1234 (Heparin_ physician_post-op)	1234 (Dr. C)	1243 (Mary J.)	4 West (Post-surgical care)	2 Feb 2005 1:00P	Accept	
1234 (Heparin_ physician_post-op)	1243 (Dr. Y)	1253 (Roberta J.)	4 West (Post-surgical care)	2 Feb 2005 12:06 PM	Accept	
1234 (Heparin_ physician_post-op)	1234 (Dr. C)	1278 (Rebecca L.)	4 West (Post-surgical care)	3 Feb 2005 12:07 PM	Reject	Aware/Will monitor
1234 (Heparin_ physician_post-op)	1543 (Dr. M)	1987 (Mary Q.)	4 West (Post-surgical care)	3 Feb 2005 12:19 PM	Closed	
1234 (Heparin_ physician_post-op)	1090 (Dr. S)	1009 (Victoria C.)	4 West (Post-surgical care)	29 Jan 2005 12:54 pm	Accept	
1234 (Heparin_ physician_post-op)	9834 (Dr. K)	1009 (Victoria C.)	3 South (Med-surg)	15 Jan 2005 1:45 PM	Reject	Patient not eligible
1234 (Heparin_ physician_post-op)	3457 (Dr. H)	0456 (Douglas C.)	3 South (Med-surg)	4 Feb 2005 2 PM	Accept	

respected individuals with domain expertise in each area. These experts review and periodically update content for which they are responsible and help address concerns that arise about this content.

Assigning an "**expiration date**" to the knowledge components of all CDS interventions can be a useful strategy to help keep the knowledge base current. These time limits should be set to correspond with the anticipated "**shelf-life**" of the intervention's knowledge and trigger content review by an appropriate domain expert after a pre-determined time since the last review has elapsed.

To ensure that alerts remain appropriate, you can keep a close eye on the use and usability issues logs in Worksheet 6-1, page 106, especially after changes to the hardware, software, or any related content. Because rules can be inter-related in

complex ways, especially as their number increases, maintaining proper performance of the entire rule set as it evolves is challenging but critical.

Because clinical decisions may be based on CDS interventions rendered using various components of an organization's collection of knowledge assets, tracking changes to the collection as expiration dates pass and updates are made becomes important to be able to understand the exact context in which an intervention was delivered. This context includes both patient data and clinical knowledge represented in information systems at the time of an intervention. Accordingly, preserving superseded knowledge, using techniques such as **versioning,** helps to link knowledge to interventions even in retrospect years after the intervention. In addition to helping an organization manage its knowledge, versioning may help people understand what happened during the course of a CDS intervention if this context ever is called into question, e.g., an allegation of malpractice regarding a decision that involved a CDS intervention. We discuss the medico-legal aspects of CDS in greater detail in Appendix B, page 117. In addition to versioning, storing other aspects of a specific intervention (e.g., recipient, patient, action taken by the recipient and reason for override of the intervention) in a log will help establish the context of the intervention.

Just as the knowledge base evolves, so do the vocabularies and coding schemes that are used to trigger and process the CDS interventions. As a result, it is important to ensure that changes to these schemas do not have adverse effects on the behavior of CDS interventions.

The Knowledge Asset Portfolio

Although not approached this way in many institutions, it is helpful to consider your organization's CDS content assets as a single portfolio of knowledge resources. These assets might exist in several different forms (e.g., material such as order sets, alerts, rules/reminders, and documentation templates) integrated into clinical information systems (e.g., CPOE and EMR). In addition, virtually all organizations have both paper-based and electronic medical reference information available for clinicians and patients that also should be considered. This universe of local content assets may come from a variety of sources, including internal content experts, CIS vendors (provided directly with the system or shared among their institutional users), governmental agencies and clearinghouses,[3] other healthcare institutions, publicly accessible Web sites, and commercial CDS content vendors (that can include print reference publishers).

For quality, efficiency, and cost reasons, it is useful to have a systematic approach to procuring and managing this material, not just individually, but taking into account the inter-relationships among its components as well. For example, similar content might be deployed in various CDS interventions

(e.g., alerts, reference materials and order sets) for patient safety, disease management, and performance improvement programs. An overarching perspective is necessary to ensure that there are optimal efficiencies, synergies, and consistency in evaluating, selecting, disseminating, monitoring, and maintaining this information.

Sudden and dramatic changes in practice, such as the withdrawal from the market of a widely used drug[4, 5] or the announcement of practice-altering clinical trial results,[6] highlight the importance of a systematic approach to managing the organization's overall CDS knowledge portfolio. These changes necessitate corresponding updates to pertinent components of the entire suite of CDS interventions, which your knowledge management mechanisms should enable in a timely and efficient manner. Otherwise, the credibility of specific CDS interventions, and the overall CDS program, can be called into question by end users. This can occur, for example, when a CDS intervention presents a user with a particular medication as the drug of choice in a particular situation after that drug has been withdrawn from the market.

As illustrated in Figures 1-2 and 1-3, leadership committees will define enterprise-wide strategies, clinical standards, and performance measures. They should likewise define a focal point of responsibility for the overall portfolio of CDS interventions used to address these. In larger organizations, roles such as the medical/nursing director of information systems and/or a clinical decision support committee might assume responsibility for the CDS content portfolio.

In any case, a coordinating function should work closely with a variety of other stakeholders and positions to manage the individual elements and overall value of the organization's CDS content assets. These individuals include subject matter experts in the clinical domains covered by the CDS interventions, the IT groups responsible for developing and deploying the interventions, and the committees and positions responsible for the intervention effects (e.g., pharmacy and therapeutics committee, quality/safety

Figure 6-3: Questions to consider about organizational knowledge management

- What intervention types are deployed throughout the enterprise?

- How many of each type is deployed and what domains/topics are covered?

- What are the content sources, monitoring/maintenance plans,* and effects of each intervention?

- Are the clinical information and recommendations consistent across interventions?[†]

- Is there an appropriate balance of content that is developed locally, shared, obtained from free sources, and purchased from commercial vendors?

- How do subject matter experts and CDS implementation staff collaborate on determining and implementing the above steps, and communicating with leadership?

- Is available CDS content optimally leveraged to meet CDS goals given available CIS infrastructure?

- How are individuals (e.g., subject matter experts) compensated for their role in maintaining the knowledge assets?

- Is there an audit trail for what decisions are made about the content assets, and why and how they are made? Who maintains this trail, and how is that done?

- What tools is the organization using to manage its repository of content assets[‡] (e.g., for authoring, storing, updating, and editing content, and tracking changes)? Who is responsible for these tools and how are content versions managed?

officer, benefits realization team). These relationships in your institution can be documented on a customized version of Figures 1-2 and 1-3. Whether or not you do this, it is helpful to have a clear picture of these functions and how they inter-relate in your organization.

Figure 6-3 contains questions that these positions and committees can consider in setting up and/or refining the organization's knowledge management approach. Some of the data to help answer these questions can be gleaned from worksheets completed in previous chapters. Worksheets 6-1 and 6-3 can be used to document issues you uncover. You can also create your own worksheets, if desired, to document and analyze this important information, and use it for knowledge management planning.

WORKSHEETS

Step 1: Assess intervention use and usability on an ongoing basis.

Feedback channels carefully developed and used during earlier steps in this book have hopefully served you well for optimizing interventions in the period surrounding their launch. Worksheet 5-4, page 96, used for tracking initial user issues and their resolution, may be filled with the rough spots that often accompany initial rollout and use. At

---

* Including department/subject matter expert responsible for the content and schedule for evaluating and updating knowledge components.

[†] This can be particularly important when content for inter-related interventions comes from different sources. Drug dosing information should be consistent across alerts and reference material used by doctors, nurses, pharmacists, and patients, to ensure consistent information and practice throughout the organization.

[‡] Professional content management tools, as opposed to spreadsheets and word processing documents, are used by commercial content developers and likewise recommended for healthcare organizations that do any significant amount of local content development.

some point, a steady state will be reached and attention can turn to assessing and improving routine intervention use. The basic structure of Worksheet 5-4 can be used for tracking this maintenance state; a modified version with sample data is presented below as Worksheet 6-1.

Quantifying how often each intervention is utilized provides a backdrop for examining its effectiveness in achieving target objectives. This usage might be assessed somewhat differently for each intervention type. For example, many different indicators of alerting activity are outlined above and in Appendix D, page 121. Some of this information can be gathered automatically (depending on clinical information system and CDS system functionality). An electronic file can be used to record logistical details about the firing of an unsolicited alert or recommendation and a user's response to it, as in Figure 6-2.

For user-initiated interventions such as order sets, documentation templates, and in-context links to reference materials (e.g., infobuttons), related quantities of interest might include the number of times users had the opportunity to select the intervention and the percent of those instances where they did so.

Ideally, the usage data can be gleaned automatically and easily from the underlying CIS, but often this is not the case. Approaches that combine automated statistics with data from surveys and surrogate markers may be needed. For example, use of an infobutton link to drug prescribing information from a CPOE medication order entry screen can be described by the number of times users clicked the link in relation to the number of patient encounters for which the CPOE was used during a given period of time. This information can be combined with survey data about how often users report obtaining information from the link that affects management decisions. Together, these data provide a picture of intervention use and impact that can inform subsequent efforts to further improve both. Qualitative feedback adds context and richness to the quantitative data. It can reveal issues with intervention content and delivery, as well as user perceptions of the intervention and its value.

A wide variety of strategies can be used to address concerns and improvement opportunities uncovered. These include additional training or communication, tweaks or major changes to the intervention content or delivery, task groups assigned to further investigate issues and develop solutions, and so forth. For example, if an important alert seems to be producing more trouble than benefit, it might be desirable to turn it off while exploring how to improve the situation. Depending on the underlying CIS delivering the alert, it may be possible to turn it off only for a given clinician, care site, or group of patients for which it is particularly problematic. Any intervention that yields more costs and problems than benefit despite reasonable remediation efforts probably should be discarded in favor of an alternative CDS approach to the objective, or a reassessment of the objective. Both can be aided by retracing a path through this book.

Do not forget to fully leverage the champions and stakeholders you have cultivated up to this point in resolving issues. For example, if there is significant controversy about new alerts or high recipient rejection of them, user champions can serve as an important bridge between other users and the implementation team in reaching a widely acceptable resolution.

By its nature, Worksheet 6-1 is a reactive document, i.e., it is used to respond to issues raised by users and others. Some of these issues will likely pertain to intervention content, for example, where users feel some aspect of the content such as currency or appropriateness is not right. In parallel with this responsive content-related work, be sure to attend to the proactive content maintenance tasks as outlined in the discussion above.

Step 2: Evaluate intervention impact on target objectives.

In some respects, this step is the bottom line for this whole book and your entire CDS program. The substantial efforts in both instances are directed

Worksheet 6-1:

Use and usability issues log

In the first column, list all the interventions that are in active clinical use. In the second column, synthesize data from all the various feedback channels. Include both quantitative information about how often users interact with the intervention and their qualitative comments about its use and impact. Including the source for the feedback can be useful if additional details about the issue are needed from the person(s) who raised it. Documenting the feedback channel can be helpful in checking on the use and usefulness of the various channels in place. For example, remediation plans can be directed as needed by the implementation team toward overuse or under use of specific channels.

The third column logs the date that the issue first surfaced or the usage data was gathered. These dates can be helpful in assessing the rate at which the implementation team is addressing the various issues, and in documenting usage trends over time (e.g., through multiple rows for the intervention, each with usage statistics and corresponding observation date). In some cases, it can be helpful to plot this data on a graph to show changes in intervention usage over time, perhaps overlaying communications and training events to demonstrate their effect.

As in Worksheet 5-4, page 96, a remediation plan for each major issue should be developed and documented. In the last column you can assign relative priorities for addressing the issue, using a scale that seems appropriate. This prioritization can help guide resource allocation and remediation schedule and is driven by a variety of factors. These include the risk to patient care of not correcting the problem, the number of users affected, the resources and time required for the fix, and the like. These relative priorities can change over time as resources such as personnel change and other interventions develop new usage issues.

This is a working document. Successfully resolved issues can be removed (ideally archived elsewhere with the date they were resolved) and new issues can be added as they occur.

Intervention Name	Usage and Usability Issues (Source/Channel)	Date Noted	Remediation Plan (Responsible Party, Date Resolved)	Priority
Heparin post-op alert	Avg. 20 firings/day across all deployed units; 30% rejection rate. High user dissatisfaction (Anne M.).	1 Mar 2005	Analysis in progress to add in better data on contraindications for heparin therapy. Alert removed from production awaiting resolution (5 Mar 2005).	Medium
PTT order set	Avg. 16 uses/day; No issues noted; good user satisfaction.	1 Apr 2005	NA	NA

Worksheet 6-1 *continued*

PTT alert	Avg. 50 firings/day; 80% rejection rate. Nurses do not feel that it is accurate and don't have time to contact physicians after it fires.	1 Apr 2005	Consider removing the intervention.	High
Heparin post-op order set	Avg. 13 uses/day; no issues noted.	1 Apr 2005	NA	NA

toward realizing measurable and important improvements in targeted healthcare processes and outcomes. The targets were initially identified in Chapter 1 (Worksheet 1-2) and then refined and validated in Chapter 4 (Worksheet 4-1). Worksheet 6-2, below, is the reckoning: How well have investments in the CDS program paid the anticipated dividends? Consider the full range of potential benefits that might have accrued from the interventions (e.g., as outlined in Figure 1-9 page 13).

To the greatest extent possible, the assessments should be quantitative and compared to baseline measurements. Ideally, you have a benefits realization team in place charged with gathering and analyzing the needed data, and reporting the results. Getting the needed quantitative information can be difficult for some improvements and may require a combination of strategies. These can include extracting data through various reporting mechanisms from the organization's clinical, administrative, and financial databases. These systems often produce standard reports or have query tools, though some data might still need to be processed manually. Keep in mind that key definitions might vary across these systems, making it difficult to create a unified picture of intervention effects. For example, if medical conditions are defined differently in financial and clini-

cal systems, it might be problematic to assess the financial implications of specific clinical changes. Healthcare data analysis vendors and consultants have experience with such complexities and can also help generate the needed measurement information.

Because there can be several interventions focused on a single clinical objective, it is important to keep straight whether the targets and performance measures pertain to the objective or to a component intervention. For example, a clinical objective might be to improve monitoring of patients receiving IV heparin, so that 95% of patients on this therapy receive the indicated monitoring.* A physician order set that makes it easier to include this testing with other orders might be one useful CDS intervention to accomplish this. However, the compliance target for this intervention might be less than 100% (e.g., if only a fraction of physicians are using CPOE). Thus, targets and baselines for objectives and the corresponding interventions need to be considered and evaluated separately. Improved compliance with the intervention is expected to improve performance toward the clinical objective. However, this should

---

* 100% might not be a reasonable target for many objectives (e.g., because there are often extenuating circumstances for a small percent of patients that would preclude them from being managed according to the objective).

not be taken for granted because a variety of factors can decouple these changes.

Enhancements assessed qualitatively are also important and should be documented as well. For example, user-perceived improvements in workflow, confidence in decision making and appreciation for the "clinical safety net" are all desirable intervention effects worth noting.

Be aware that careful benefits measurement is often time consuming and costly, and relatively few organizations currently do it very well. Considering these measurement issues early in working with your CIS infrastructure and developing the CDS interventions hopefully helped optimize your access to needed measurement data. As CIS and CDS systems evolve further, especially in light of pay-for-performance trends, this data should become easier to obtain.

Do not necessarily expect to fully achieve your goals on the first measurement round. Progress will depend on a variety of factors, including time between measurements. Establish reasonable measurement intervals and expectations for improvement speed based on input from key stakeholders. If formal accountability for realizing CDS benefits has been assigned (e.g., with implications for job performance assessment or departmental budgeting), then care and collaboration in setting and measuring these benefits becomes particularly critical. Again, it might be ideal for a benefits realization team to handle this.

Step 3: Continually enhance the value to users and impact on goals and objectives of individual CDS interventions and the overall CDS program.

Worksheet 6-1 provides a micro-level view of use and usability issues. Worksheet 6-2 provides an analogous detailed view of intervention performance. Complementing these detailed perspectives with a higher-level overview can help in formulating CDS program enhancement strategies.

Worksheet 6-3 builds on data from the two previous worksheets to provide this overview. It allows you to evaluate intervention status and make enhancement plans in light of higher-level goals and objectives (e.g., those originally explored in Figure 1-5 and Worksheets 1-1 and 1-2). Individual use and usability issues for each intervention are synthesized in this light into a strategy that will help drive the next round of CDS program enhancement (and iteration through the steps in this book).

Worksheet 6-2:
Performance against objectives

This worksheet is anchored in the first column with a list of all clinical objectives addressed by interventions launched within your CDS program. These, together with data for the following four columns, can be brought forward from the version of Worksheet 4-1, page 79, that you have created for each intervention. Note that a single clinical objective might be followed by several rows of interventions if a set was implemented to address the objective. When documenting baseline performance and desired and actual improvement, make sure you are clear on whether these pertain to the specific desired action targeted by the intervention, or to the broader objective.

In the sixth column, record the measured progress toward the key target of interest, and in the seventh column, record the related positive intervention effects.

Clinical Objective	Desired Action	Intervention Name	Baseline Performance	Desired Improvement	Actual Performance Improvement	Other Effects
Improve heparin prophylaxis in post-op patients	Increase orders for post-op heparin prophylaxis	Heparin post-op order set	62% compliance	100% for patients without contra-indications	85% compli-ance in follow up (not yet able to reli-ably exclude patients with contraindica-tions)	Users indicated intervention had a posi-tive effect on workflow; com-plained when it was briefly unavailable
		Heparin post-op alert	71% compliance		90% compliance	Users dislike the alert so that many more have begun to use the order set
Improve monitoring of heparin for patients on IV heparin	Increase PTT orders for patients prescribed IV heparin	PTT order set	88% compliance		92% compliance	None
	Increase collec-tion of PTT by nursing	PTT alert	66% compliance		94% compliance	Alert has been accompanied by training that has improved compliance

Worksheet 6-3:

CDS program enhancement plans

To fill in the first column, go back to the top of each Worksheet 1-2, page 19, and copy the high level clinical goals from any worksheet that contains an objective for which you developed an intervention. While you are revisiting the worksheets prepared from Chapter 1, be on the lookout for other CDS goals or high-level clinical objectives that might be appropriate to add to the scope of your CDS program. In fact, if and when your organization is ready to contemplate significant program enhancements, you can actually begin the next pass through all the steps in this book.

For now, copy the clinical objectives and intervention names from Worksheet(s) 4-1, page 79, into the second and third columns of Worksheet 6-3. The effectiveness summary in the fourth column is a synthesis of the last two columns from Worksheet 6-2. The Issues and Usability summary synthesizes the major issues and opportunities uncovered in Worksheet 6-1.

The last column is the punch line for this worksheet. It presents an overview of the next major steps in your CDS program. It should begin to outline a plan for improving intervention acceptance and use among recipients, and effectiveness in achieving target objectives. You can also begin noting additional interventions that might help achieve objectives, as well as additional objectives and goals to tackle based on ongoing dialogue with other stakeholders and any capability enhancements to underlying CIS infrastructure.

High-level Clinical Goal	Clinical Objective	Intervention Name	Effectiveness Summary	Issues and Usability Summary	Enhancement Plans
Improve anticoagulation use					Given success of initial interventions, will add enoxaparin guidelines as objective for next round CDS
	Improve heparin prophylaxis in post-op patients	Heparin post-op order set	Moderate—9% improvement		None
		Heparin post-op alert	High—19% improvement		Add the prophylaxis order to the alert. The action on the alert may improve user satisfaction

Worksheet 6-3 *continued*

	Improve monitoring of PTT in patients on IV heparin	PTT order set	Low—4% but baseline was relatively high.		Add header above the PTT order to make it easier to see
		PTT alert	Very high—28% improvement		Improvements may have been related to increased awareness and in-services, remove alert for now with careful monitoring of compliance

CONCLUDING COMMENTS

Like the previous chapter, this final step in this book is both an end and a beginning. The sequential process outlined in the six chapters can be iteratively repeated to continuously improve the contribution the CDS program makes to your organization's clinical and business performance.

The content, technology, and implementation procedures on which CDS programs depend are at a relatively early stage of development. As a result, there are few robust models for successful program deployment that can be easily emulated. As the field matures and these components become more widespread, successive CDS implementations will build on richer foundations. For example, emerging certification programs and standards for more sophisticated content and intervention delivery technology will likely lead to more readily available and easily implemented CDS interventions in the near future.

The authors view this second edition as validation of our initial plan to provide a continually evolving resource that we hope will better meet the needs of healthcare organizations over time. We welcome your participation in the effort and hope you will send us feedback on this edition, share your experiences and insights with your colleagues and us, and consider joining the HIMSS CDS Task Force as a forum for these activities.

References

1   Ash JS, Berg M, Coiera E. Some unintended consequences of information technology in health care: the nature of patient care information system-related errors. *JAMIA*. 2004 Mar-Apr;11(2):104–12.

2   Hsieh TC, Kuperman GJ, Jaggi T, et al. Characteristics and consequences of drug allergy alert overrides in a computerized physician order entry system. *JAMIA*. 2004 Nov-Dec;11(6):482–91.

3   E.g., National Guideline Clearinghouse (http://www.ngc.gov), National Quality Measures Clearinghouse (http://www.qualitymeasures.ahrq.gov/).

4   Oberholzer-Gee F, Inamdar SN. Merck's recall of Rofecoxib—a strategic perspective. *N Engl J Med*. 2004;Nov 18;351(21):2147–9.

5   Responding to the Rofecoxib withdrawal crisis: a new model for notifying patients at risk and their health care providers. *Ann Int Med*. http://www.annals.org/cgi/content/abstract/142/3/182.

6   U.S. Food and Drug Administration. 2003 Safety Alert - Serevent (salmeterol xinafoate). Available at: http://www.fda.gov/medwatch/SAFETY/2003/serevent.htm.

Additional Web Reading and Resources

•   Doherty JA, Reichley RM, Noirot LA, et al. Monitoring pharmacy expert system performance using statistical process control methodology. *AMIA Proceedings*. 2003;205–9.

•   Jenders RA, Huang H, Hripcsak G, Clayton PD. Evolution of a knowledge base for a clinical decision support system encoded in the Arden Syntax. *AMIA Proceedings*. 1998:558–62. This article illustrates the substantial work required to maintain clinical knowledge bases. For example, in their 156 Medical Logic Modules developed over 78 months, the authors noted 2,020 distinct versions that included 5,528 changed statements over time.

•   Rosenstein AH. Measuring the benefit of performance improvement and decision support. *Am J Med Qual*. 1999 Nov-Dec:14(6):262–9.

•   Shiffman RN. Guideline maintenance and revision. 50 years of the Jones criteria for diagnosis of rheumatic fever. *Arch Ped Adolesc Med*. 1995 Jul;149(7):727–32. The article provides an excellent example of the types of revisions and expected reasons for revising clinical guidelines. It brings up the point that changes in clinical knowledge are not the number one reason for changes; rather, most changes are required to fix ambiguously defined concepts or outright errors in original encoding.

•   Teich JM, Pankaj R, Merchia BS, et al. Effects of computerized physician order entry on prescribing practices. *Arch Int Med*. 2000;160:2741–2747. http://archinte.ama-assn.org/cgi/content/abstract/160/18/2741.

Appendix A

Standards Pertinent to CDS

The use of standards by an information system is an important consideration when assessing your organization's information infrastructure and when considering purchasing systems and software. CDS interventions may require both data (patient-specific or institution-specific) and clinical knowledge in order to function. Standards can address both of these broad areas. Indeed, standards can play a role in a number of areas pertinent to data collection, aggregation, retrieval and interpretation.

- **Vocabulary.** By providing a unique identifier for patient-related data elements that you may wish to capture, store, and use for decision support, a vocabulary enables an organized display and retrieval of appropriate data. Many vocabularies also denote relationships among concepts. This can be used by CDS applications to retrieve related data for interpretation. Examples include SNOMED CT (clinical data: www.snomed.org), LOINC (laboratory data: www.loinc.org), and ICD9-CM (diagnosis data: www.who.int). The most relevant of these for CDS are listed in Chapter 2; a more comprehensive list is provided below in Figure A-1. Other potentially relevant standard vocabularies exist. However, some of these have been incorporated into other vocabularies. For example, a number of standard nursing vocabularies, such as the Perioperative Nursing Data Set

(PNDS), Home Health Care Classification (HHCC), and the North American Nursing Diagnosis Association (NANDA) terminology, are incorporated in SNOMED CT.

- **Messaging.** Messaging standards allow exchange of data between systems developed by different vendors without having to negotiate site-specific rules for every interface. Such standards also may govern communication between applications on the computer desktop. Examples include HL7 messaging standard (www.hl7.org), HL7 CCOW (Clinical Context Object Workgroup) standard, and NCPDP SCRIPT (pharmacy orders: www.ncpdp.org).

- **Data types/formats.** Non-textual data, such as images, may require a specialized format to ensure best resolution and to meet the display requirements of many devices. Different types of data (e.g., text and imaging) may be organized into aggregate units, such as documents, and these units also may be specified by a data type standard. Examples include DICOM (imaging data: medical.nema.org), and CDA (clinical documents: www.hl7.org).

- **Functional standards.** Instead of coding or representing data, a functional standard prescribes a set of characteristics for a system that can be used to assess a particular application. A functional standard may require the use of other standards as an operating characteristic of an information system. An example is HL7 Electronic Health Record Functional Standard and Specification (http://www.hl7.org/ehr/downloads).

- **Knowledge representation.** The logic or rules in a CDS intervention must be stored in a way that can be executed by the computer in order to provide the CDS. A knowledge representation standard specifies the form of the knowledge. Examples include Arden Syntax (alerts/reminders: www.hl7.org) and Guideline Elements Model (GEM) (guidelines: www.astm.org).

- **Data model.** This provides a blueprint for organization of data (e.g., a database schema that is used to aggregate and store data in a data warehouse or central data repository). Such a model, providing standard classes and attributes of data, also can be used to construct standard messages to transmit data. Example: HL7 Reference Information Model.

- **Expression language.** This may include the way that queries are represented, providing a standard mechanism for retrieving data from repositories. An expression language also may include a standard format for logical statements, and these can be used to interpret data in order to provide CDS interventions. An example is HL7 GELLO (in the process of being approved as a standard).

An overall information system for a typical organization is constructed from a collection of many applications, each of which serves a particular function (e.g., billing system, electronic health record, results review system, laboratory information system). Such systems may come from different vendors. Use of standards covering the above areas helps to ensure that data captured, manipulated, stored, or transmitted by one system can be exchanged with and used by other systems, thus facilitating system and data integration. Conversely, the absence of standards means that idiosyncratic, site-specific interfaces must be developed to

exchange data between any two systems—a substantial challenge considering the number of different applications that can be used in a healthcare organization. In addition, interpretation software would have to be developed for each separate application so that those data could be used by other applications, such as those that process CDS interventions. Thus, the use of standards reduces the cost of creating, integrating, and maintaining information systems and their CDS functions.

While standards can be valuable, the use of standards does not eliminate the need for site-specific engineering. There will always be local concepts and identifiers that require capture or storage, and system interfaces may need to exchange data in a particular way to meet a local need. However, linking such local requirements with standards (e.g., mapping a local laboratory test code to a standard vocabulary concept) will aid in the aggregation and exchange of data needed to provide robust CDS interventions.

Standards may arise through several mechanisms. A company with a dominant market share in a particular type of application may produce a de facto standard. A government agency with regulatory authority in a particular domain may mandate the use of formalisms. Less formally, a group of professional organizations or software vendors may choose independently to endorse a standard. However, the most important mechanism currently used for the creation, promulgation, and maintenance of standards is the standards development organization (SDO). SDOs include not only broad-based groups that sponsor many different standards related to healthcare computing but also groups that are focused on specific domains, such as imaging.

Health Level 7 is an international SDO for healthcare computing (HL7: www.hl7.org). It is organized as a collection of technical committees, each addressing a specific standard or part of a standard, using a consensus method of development and a formal set of rules for reviewing and approving any new standard. Other SDOs that produce standards regarding healthcare computing include the American Society

Figure A-1: Some standard vocabularies

Vocabulary	Coverage
Systemized Nomenclature Of Medicine Clinical Terms (SNOMED-CT)	Multiple areas
International Classification of Diseases Clinical Modification (ICD-9-CM, ICD-10-CM)	Diagnoses
Current Procedural Terminology (CPT-4)	Procedures
Logical Observation Identifiers Names and Codes (LOINC)	Laboratory tests
Healthcare Common Procedure Coding System (HCPCS)	Supplies, non-physician services
Code on Dental Procedures and Nomenclature (CDT)	Procedures
National Drug Codes (NDC)	Drugs: Names
Human Genome Nomenclature (HUGN)	Genetics
EPA Substance Registry System (SRS)	Non-medicinal chemicals
RxNorm	Drugs: Names + dose forms
National Drug File-Reference Terminology (NDF-RT)	Drugs: Mechanism of action, physiologic effects
Health Insurance Portability and Accountability Act code sets (HIPAA)	Billing, administrative functions
Health Level 7	Demographics and others
Registry of Toxic Effects of Chemical Substances (RTECS)	Toxic chemicals
Chemical Abstract Service (CAS) Numbers	Chemicals
International Classification for Nursing Practice (ICNP)	Nursing
Immunization Data Transactions (HL7)	Vaccines and manufacturers
U.S. Food and Drug Administration/Center for Drug Evaluation and Research (FDA/CDER) Data Standards Manual	Manufactured drug dosage form, package information
Diagnostic Related Groups (DRG)	Diagnoses
Global Medical Device Nomenclature (GMDN)	Medical devices
Universal Medical Device Nomenclature System (UMDNS)	Medical devices
Medical Dictionary for Regulatory Activities (MedDRA)	Medical product regulations
DIG35	Image metadata
Medcin	Clinical terms

for Testing and Materials (ASTM: www.astm.org), Comité Européen de Normalisation (CEN: www.cenorm.be), and the Clinical Data Interchange Standards Consortium (CDISC: www.cdisc.org).

Besides its messaging standard, HL7 also sponsors a variety of other standards pertinent to CDS interventions. These include a standard for interprocess communication of user and patient contexts among desktop applications (CCOW); a specification for clinical documents, the Clinical Document Architecture (CDA); a formalism for communication with vocabulary servers, the Clinical

Terminology Services (CTS) standard; a standard data model, the Reference Information Model or RIM, which will be the basis for all version 3 HL7 messages; and Arden Syntax, a standard for procedural knowledge representation of the clinical "rules" used to encode the knowledge base of a CDSS. HL7 also is developing an expression language standard (Guideline Execution Language or GELLO) and is working on a standard for representing clinical practice guidelines. Also under development are standards for infobuttons and order sets. Finally, HL7 has produced a functional standard that can be used to assess the quality of electronic health records, the EHR Functional Model and Specification (www.hl7.org/ehr/downloads).

Appendix B

Medico-legal Considerations with CDS

Legal issues often are cited as an important consideration in the implementation of CDS interventions and even as an outright barrier to their implementation. The most important aspect of the challenge lies in the concern regarding malpractice liability, while issues related to government regulation of software are comparatively less important. Regarding legal liability, a commonly expressed concern is that use of a CDS application will increase liability exposure for clinicians and healthcare organizations. The mechanism for this increased liability is felt to be CDS interventions, such as alerts and reminders that are ignored by clinicians, which in turn might be used to support an allegation of malpractice.

This fear has been addressed in a number of ways. Some organizations have inactivated logging of CDS interventions, thus removing this source of documentation that might be discoverable in a legal action. Others keep such logs but explicitly declare them to be outside the official medical record (e.g., as part of quality improvement initiatives) and thus, theoretically, not discoverable. It is questionable, though, whether such information could be prevented from legal discovery.

Because some studies demonstrate a high rate of false-positive alerting[1] (e.g., in CPOE systems), providing a mechanism for the clinician receiving the alert to declare that a CDS intervention is incorrect or otherwise not applicable to specific patient may help in defending against malpractice allegations.

Others have advocated that mechanisms be put into place to make it more difficult for clinicians to override very high priority alerts, and for improving the signal to noise ratio of alerts.

Knowledge management techniques, which were discussed in Chapter 6, help preserve the context of a specific CDS intervention, including the state of the CDS content at the time an intervention about a specific patient was delivered. If questions are raised about a clinician's decision involving a CDS intervention, say in a malpractice allegation, these techniques may help establish the exact context of the intervention and may help others understand why a particular decision was made.

An important consideration in addressing the concern over a possible increase in legal liability is that malpractice is defined as a violation of a standard of care and that the standard of care may vary by region. Some have suggested that the use of CDS in a given area may generally increase the standard of clinical care because of the evidence in the medical literature that the use of such systems can improve the quality of care and reduce medical errors. Thus, in this point of view, not having a CDS program in place may increase malpractice liability because its absence might be cited in a legal action as evidence that an organization did not use available technology to try to prevent harm to a patient.

Further reassurance regarding the use of CDS interventions is expected to come from the establishment of standards of quality for software systems and knowledge bases and certification efforts based on such standards (see discussion in Chapter 1). These quality efforts may emphasize the need to test and maintain the knowledge contained in CDS in order to minimize errors on the part of the systems themselves.

Nevertheless, considerable uncertainty attends commentary regarding legal liability and CDS. Standards related to such liability often are determined by case law, and CDS interventions thus far have not been a factor in malpractice litigation. Thus, it is difficult to ascertain with certainty how the presence of a CDS intervention, or such specific factors as access to its output logs, actually influence liability.

Other legal concerns arise when knowledge is shared. For example, while the benefits (such as reduced cost of knowledge engineering and dissemination of best practices) are recognized, organizations that create knowledge bases for CDS are often reluctant to share them, in part because of concern that the authors of such knowledge may be held legally liable for its use at a different institution. Again, there is a dearth of case law to address these concerns, but some cite the "textbook exception" and the typical legal regime that makes an individual practitioner responsible for his or her actions, regardless of how the practitioner arrived at those actions

(e.g., via use of a CDS intervention). Medical textbooks typically contain such a disclaimer, but again this has not been tested in litigation with regard to other CDS systems.

This book outlines a careful approach to developing, deploying and monitoring CDS interventions. Though not intended in any way to represent legal advice, this approach hopefully will be a useful component of your organization's efforts to address any legal risks associated with CDS.

References

1 Payne TH, Nichol WP, Hoey P, Savarino J. Characteristics and override rates of order checks in a practitioner order entry system. *AMIA Proceedings.* 2002;602–6.

Additional Reading and Resources

• Berner ES. Ethical and legal issues in the use of clinical decision support systems. *JHIM.* 2002:16:34–37.

• Fox J, Thomson R. Clinical decision support systems: a discussion of quality, safety and legal liability issues. *AMIA Proceedings.* 2002;265–269.

• Miller RA. Legal issues related to medical decision support systems. *Int J Clin Monit Comput.* 1989;6(2):75–80.

• Miller RA, Gardner RM. Recommendations for responsible monitoring and regulation of clinical software systems. *JAMIA.* 1997;4:442–457.

• Scherpbier HJ, Klein SR, Perreault LE, Jenders RA. Aspects of knowledge-sharing using the Arden Syntax. *HIMSS Proceedings.* 1996;2:110–122.

Appendix C

Pilot Site Selection

As discussed in the section on intervention rollout in Chapter 5, page 90, CDS interventions that are highly complex or disruptive to workflow (e.g., complex clinical pathways) should often be introduced into large health systems in a phased approach. This can help implementers identify and rectify major problems before involving hundreds or thousands of recipients.

An incremental launch raises the question of where to start. Although there is not much literature focusing on this issue specifically for CDS, discussions of the related issue of pilot site selection for CIS implementations are emerging. Traditionally, the rationale for selecting these pilot sites for complex CIS initiatives is drawn from the following lines of reasoning:

- Site A has the greatest chances of success.
- New York, NY Strategy: Site B is the most challenging area in which to work ... If we can succeed here, we can succeed anywhere.
- Academic Strategy: The only way to really evaluate the impact of the interventions is to randomly select a set of sites and use the rest as controls.
- Hawaii Strategy: Site C is the smallest and the most removed site. If we fail here, it will not hurt the organization very badly.
- Midtown, America Strategy: Site D. Select the site most representative of the entire organization.
- Keep friends close, enemies closer, strategy: Site E. Select the site with the most vocal and influential naysayer on the premise that if you can convince this person, he/she will become your best supporter.
- Site F. Select the site that has the most to gain from the implementation of the system.
- Site G. Select the site that "wants" to do it the most.

Against a backdrop of reported problematic CIS implementations,[1] investigators have proposed a "Success Factor Profile" (SFP) to help organizations select the pilot site that is most likely to succeed and establish a solid foundation for organization-wide rollout.[2] The SFP identified the following five key success indicators, which are also pertinent to selecting pilot sites for complex CDS intervention launches:

- **Innovation history:** the clinical unit or area's record of innovation leadership and previous pilot program success;
- **Generalizability:** relevant gains for the rest of the organization from the products and processes developed with the pilot area;
- **Innovation "personality":** enthusiasm to pilot new tools and processes; resources for inevitable struggles; strength of the leadership team;
- **Learning opportunities:** quality feedback for development and implementation teams to improve products and processes; and
- **Success likelihood:** probability of prosperous development and implementation of new tools and processes.

Some detailed data about the potential pilot sites can provide further insights into these success factors for each. These items are listed below.

- The clinical unit or area's "vital signs"
  - Number of beds (or examination rooms)
  - Types of patients cared for
  - Average daily census (or number of patients seen per day)
  - Average length of stay (or average visit time)
  - Admission, discharge, and transfer activity
  - Number of employees
  - Composition of the workforce on a "typical" day
  - Staff stability (turnover and use of supplemental staff)
  - Identity and roles of key leadership personnel
  - Unit operations
  - Patient care documentation
  - Unique site operations
  - Current technologic efforts underway
  - Site encapsulation
- Information infrastructure
  - Existing hardware
  - Existing software
  - Unique hardware/software
- "Peopleware"
  - Staff experience with and affinity for technology
  - Staff previous responses to change
  - Predicted responses to technologic change
  - History with technologic change
  - Current and potential technological change champions
- Innovation Prospects
  - Largest benefit anticipated from electronic transformation
  - Biggest drawback anticipated from transformation
  - Additional hardware needs
  - Resources for the change
  - Barriers and challenges likely to be encountered
  - Desire to be a pilot site
  - Technology "wish list"

Unfortunately, there is no simple formula for determining which pilot site is most likely to be the most helpful for a successful rollout of complex CIS or CDS systems. However, the considerations outlined above can help inform this decision.

References

1 Massaro TA. Introducing physician order entry at a major academic medical center: I. Impact on organizational culture and behavior. *Acad Med.* 1993;68(1):20–5.

2 Lorenzi NM, Smith JB, Conner SR, Campion TR. Related articles, links to the success factor profile for clinical computer innovation. *Medinfo.* 2004;2004:1077–80.

Appendix D

Additional Statistics and Reports for Evaluating Alerts

Reports about alert firing and user response can provide useful insights for ensuring that the alerts achieve their intended goals efficiently and effectively. The following reports and statistics illustrate the broad spectrum of intervention firing-related data that can be gleaned and how it might be used.

The ability to easily generate all the measures described below is certainly not widespread, and may not be fully available in any one organization or system. Nonetheless, some of these measures might be accessible in your environment and worth pursuing to help identify potential alerting problem areas. They might also help stimulate further research and development in this important area.

Figure D-1 is an example of a clinical alert monitoring report that organizations might generate on a monthly or quarterly basis. Each of the alert types that are currently used in the clinical setting are presented, along with the number of times they have been displayed, the rate at which they are firing, the percentage of time they are overridden, and an estimate of their overall burden on the end users. See below for a detailed definition of each calculation.

This type of report provides a window into the interplay between the alert and users. For example, there has been a significant change in alert firing in the "drugs in the elderly" category (i.e., percent change in alert frequency is 100%). One cannot tell solely from this report whether the change was caused by the way this group of alerts is firing (i.e., a

change in triggering data), a change in the ordering patterns of clinicians, or even that these alerts just went into production. Clearly, any changes of this magnitude would warrant investigation.

One might also be interested in looking at potential reasons for the high **alert override rate** in the drug-drug interaction category. To accomplish this, one would need to "drill down" into this category and begin reviewing the override rates of each of the individual alerts that comprise this category (see Figure D-2, for example).

Calculations
Alert frequency
The total number of times the alert has been displayed.

Alert frequency change
The percent change in the alert frequency between the previous measuring interval and the current measuring interval.

Alert rate
The number of alerts presented divided by the number of alert opportunities. The number of alert opportunities is based on the number of times each patient's electronic data was accessed in such a manner that if an alert was present that it would have been presented. Therefore, the number of alert opportunities is related to how the alert presentation mechanism interacts with the clinician's workflow. Clearly, if the alert rate is too high, one would want to adjust the

Figure D-1: Clinical alert monitoring report, Oct. 1, 2004–Oct. 31, 2004

Report 1 Clinical Alert Monitoring Report for Oct. 1, 2004 to Oct. 31, 2004

Alert type	Alert Frequency	AF Change	Alert Rate	AR Change	Override Rate	OR Change	Alert Burden	AB Change
Health maintenance	345	−6%	8%	2%	43%	3%	148.4	4%
Drug-drug interaction	326	3%	5%	−4%	78%	−3%	254.3	−4%
Corollary orders	124	23%	4%	6%	29%	5%	36.0	2%
Drugs in elderly	32	100%	9%	100%	17%	100%	5.4	100%
Renal dose adjustments	43	−3%	14%	2%	9%	−2%	3.9	−5%
Totals	870	6%	7%	4%	51%	4%	447.9	4%

Figure D-2: Drug-drug interaction alert monitoring report, Oct. 1, 2004–Oct. 31, 2004

Alert Name	Alert Frequency	AF Change	Alert Rate	AR Change	Override Rate	OR Change	Alert Burden	AB Change
Warfarin/sulfa	345	−6%	8%	2%	43%	3%	148.4	4%
Viagra/nitrates	326	3%	5%	−4%	78%	−3%	254.3	−4%
Ace inhibitors/potassium supplements	124	23%	4%	6%	29%	5%	36.0	2%
Digoxin/Amiodarone	32	100%	9%	100%	17%	100%	5.4	100%
Broncho-dilators/quinolones	43	−3%	14%	2%	9%	−2%	3.9	−5%
Totals	870	6%	7%	4%	51%	4%	447.9	4%

alert presentation mechanism to reduce the potential number of alert presentation opportunities.

For example, in the case of "health maintenance" reminders, one could choose to present any applicable health maintenance reminders every time a clinician opened the patient's chart. While such a system would certainly increase the possibility of a clinician actually seeing the alert, it may annoy clinicians who are simply looking up patient information following the patient visit (i.e., when the patient is not in the vicinity of the clinician). Therefore, one might decide to reduce the number of alert opportunities by changing the presentation mechanism in such a way that the alerts are only presented to the patient's primary care clinician when a new clinical encounter is created or when that encounter is closed.

Similarly, the number of medication orders transmitted to the pharmacy could approximate the number of alert opportunities for drug-drug interaction alerts. Clearly, this number would be a slight underestimate of the total number of alert opportunities since it would not take into account those ordering sessions during which an alert was presented and the clinician chose to end the session without entering any orders. Therefore, a better estimate of the total number of drug-drug interaction alert opportunities would be the number of times a medication name was entered into the system and the drug-drug interaction checking module was activated.

Alert rate (AR) change

The percent change in the alert rate between the previous measuring interval and the current measuring interval.

$$\text{Alert Rate Change} = \frac{100 * (\text{Current Alert Rate} - \text{Previous Alert Rate})}{\text{Previous Alert Rate}}$$

Alert override rate

The number of instances in which the clinician chooses not to accept the alert's recommendation divided by the total number of times the alert was presented. In many instances a clinician may "override" the alert when it is initially presented and then decide to follow the recommendation at some point later on in the same clinical encounter. One approach is to calculate the alert override rate based on whether the alert is still "valid" (i.e., the recommended actions have not been carried out) after 12 hours.

Conversely, one could choose to focus on the positive aspects of the alerts and present the **alert acceptance rate,** which is the number of times the alert's suggestion was followed or accepted divided by the total number of times the alert was presented. Once again, this could be accomplished by checking for the action recommended by the alert over a 12-hour period.

Alert override rate change

The percent change in the alert override rate between the previous measuring interval and the current measuring interval.

Alert burden

The alert frequency multiplied by the override rate. The alert burden is designed to indicate how often a particular alert, or group of alerts, is being presented to clinicians and is judged not to be of use (evidenced by the fact that the clinician chose to override the alert) for any number of reasons.

Alert burden change

The percent change in the alert burden between the previous measuring interval and the current measuring interval.

Totals

The alert frequency and the alert burden totals are the sums of the items in each column. All the other column totals depict the weighted means (based on the alert frequency) for all the values in the column.

In addition to these high-level reports, one could also utilize reports that contain the information below. Such reports could be generated from the log file described in Figure 6-2. Considerations for interpreting the results are also discussed.

Total number of alerts of all types generated per patient per visit for outpatients or during day for inpatients

More than 10 alerts per day could indicate that patient is very ill, has not been seen for a long time, or that there are too many alerts in the system. Too many alerts also might suggest that there is an underlying clinical problem with the quality of care being delivered. The last potential educational deficit might best be addressed in some appropriate manner outside direct patient care activities; alerts and reminders are not an effective method to educate clinicians.[1] Nonetheless, other CDS-related interventions might be of use here, for example, enabling users to track their clinical information needs[2] or providing electronic links to pertinent knowledge resources for outside review.

Acceptance rate for each alert

Alerts or recommendations with low acceptance rates (for example, less than 50%) are candidates for further investigation. Keep in mind that an acceptance rate might vary depending on the nature of the alert. High rejection rates could signify false positives or errors in alert generation, general clinician disagreement with the recommendation or insufficient appreciation of the evidence or the rationale behind it, data errors and so on. Depending on the cause, the appropriate response could be reassessing alert triggers, providing additional education to clinicians about the importance of the alert, fixing data problems, or reconsidering the appropriateness of the alert and its recommendations.[3]

Number of times each specific alert fires for each clinician over various time frames

An excessive number of alerts for any single event to a single clinician could be cause for investigation. For example, greater than five per day, 10 per week, or 20 per month of the same type of alert to the same clinician with less than 50% acceptance might indicate an opportunity to refine alert firing parameters, perhaps because there are legitimate reasons why the clinician's actions appear to contradict recommended practice. For example, an oncologist may regularly prescribe a medication in doses not routinely used by other clinicians and that would otherwise be excessive. If this is the case, it might make sense to add a parameter to the alert logic so that it never fires for specified clinicians or specialties (if the system and organizational policies allow such customization). Also, circumstances might have changed and, as a result, the alert might no longer be appropriate in general. In this case its value as a CDS intervention should be reassessed. Alternatively, it could indicate a need for further clinician education.

Acceptance rate for each alert type by physical location of the device at which the alert or recommendation was received

Elevated rejection rates or low acceptance rates at a location could indicate that the particular alert/recommendation may not be appropriate for patients or clinicians at that location. For example, a system should not send alert pages to surgeons when they are in the operating room.

Number of times each specific alert is generated each day, week and month. Sort by the most frequently occurring alerts and recommendations.

Look carefully at the most frequently and least frequently appearing alerts and recommendations. Make sure all of the most frequently occurring alerts are correct and appropriate. Make sure all the least frequently appearing are correct and worth keeping in the system. Be sensitive to patterns showing large changes in alert firings, which could indicate the need for further evaluation. For example, analysis could reveal a need to reassess alert appropriateness; identify shifts in practice patterns; or determine if software or content changes have inappropriately affected alert firing.

Worksheet 6-1, page 106, can be used to document any of these issues that your data uncover during ongoing evaluation.

References

1   McDonald CJ. Protocol-based computer reminders: the quality of care and the non-perfectability of man. *New Engl J Med.* 1976 Dec 9;295(24):1351–5.

2   Ely JW, Osheroff JA, Ferguson KJ, Chambliss ML, Vinson DC, Moore JL. Lifelong self-directed learning using a computer database of clinical questions. *J Fam Prac.* 1997;45(5):383–388.

3   Doherty JA, Reichley RM, Noirot LA, et al. Monitoring pharmacy expert system performance using statistical process control methodology. *AMIA Proceedings.* 2003:205–9.

Glossary

This glossary focuses on how terms are used in this book.
Some terms may have other common definitions when used in other contexts.

active guideline: computer-based display of a clinical practice guideline in which clinical actions (e.g., order a test, administer a medication) are represented as links to a computer application (e.g., computer-based provider order entry system) that allows those actions to be ordered directly.[1]

Agency for Healthcare Research and Quality (AHRQ): An agency of the U.S. Department of Health and Human Services whose mission is to improve the quality, safety, efficiency, and effectiveness of healthcare for all Americans (www.ahrq.gov).

alert: a common type of clinical decision support intervention, typically an unsolicited message to a clinician about a patient's care or status that requires attention. For example, alerts can be used to warn of a potentially dangerous situation such as the presence of a seriously abnormal lab value, or placement of an order for a contraindicated treatment or for a medication that could produce a serious drug-drug interaction.

alert acceptance rate: the number of times the alert's suggestion was followed or accepted, divided by the total number of times the alert was presented. This can be determined by checking for the action recommended by the alert over a fixed period of time.

alert burden: how often a particular alert, or group of alerts, is being presented and judged not to be of use (evidenced by the fact that clinicians overrode the alert) for any number of reasons. The alert burden is calculated from the alert frequency multiplied by the alert override rate.

alert escalation: the process by which an alert is sent to additional people, or delivered by more urgent means, when the initial recipient of an alert has not responded appropriately (acknowledgement or clinical action) within a particular time frame.[2]

alert fatigue: the state triggered in clinicians who have been repeatedly exposed to clinical alerts and have some negative reaction (e.g., irritation, failing to respond appropriately to important notification). Alert fatigue can be increased if the alerts are deemed to be irrelevant to the current patient, arrive at an inopportune point in the clinical workflow, or are incorrect (i.e., a false positive alert).

alert override rate: the number of instances in which the clinician chooses not to accept the alert's recommendation or to perform the recommended action divided by the total number of times the alert was presented. See also **alert acceptance rate**.

application: a software program designed to perform a specific set of functions, such as retrieve recent clinical laboratory results or enable a clinician to enter a medication order.

baseline performance: a measurement of clinical processes or outcomes against which future comparisons can be made.

benefits realization: a multi-faceted process that seeks to insure that the anticipated benefits associated with implementation and use of clinical information systems and clinical decision support are achieved in an efficient manner. The process focuses on the refinement of clinical and administrative workflows, organizational policies and procedures, and changes in individual, team, and departmental roles and responsibilities.

beta testing: a phase of software or application testing of a new product or feature with selected users to discover inappropriate application behavior (e.g., bugs or incorrectly designed system features), inadequate functionality, or possible product enhancements before an application is released to the entire organization.

CDR: see **clinical data repository**.

Centers for Medicare & Medicaid Services (CMS): An agency of the U.S. Department of Health and Human Services that administers health care coverage through the Medicare, Medicaid and other programs. CMS is also responsible for administrative simplification standards from HIPAA, quality standards in healthcare facilities through its survey and certification activity, and other initiatives pertinent to CDS (www.cms.hhs.gov).

Certification Commission for Health Information Technology (CCHIT): A private-sector, voluntary initiative to certify health information technology products (www.cchit.org).

champion: a clinical decision support stakeholder outside the implementation team who is enthusiastic about a clinical decision support intervention or program and assists in its development or deployment.

clinical data repository (CDR): a database system that brings together (often in real time) clinical data from many sources, including electronic health records and ancillary systems such as laboratory information systems. A CDR typically is structured to provide a view of an individual patient's data in order to facilitate clinical care. See also **data warehouse**.

clinical decision support (CDS): refers broadly to providing clinicians or patients with clinical knowledge and patient-related information, intelligently filtered or presented at appropriate times, to enhance patient care. Clinical knowledge of interest could range from simple facts and relationships to best practices for managing patients with specific disease states, new medical knowledge from clinical research, and other types of information.

clinical decision support (CDS) goals and objectives: the target healthcare processes and outcomes that CDS efforts are intended to achieve. Goals are high-level or strategic targets, such as increasing patient safety; objectives are more specific, tactical targets, such as increasing the use of specific life-saving medications in appropriate circumstances. Figure 1-5 (page 7) and Figure 1-7 (page 9) provide some examples.

clinical decision support (CDS) intervention: involves delivering one or more specific pieces of clinical knowledge or data to an individual at a specific time and place to address a CDS objective. CDS interventions include the CDS content and the logistics (such as software applications and workflow processes) by which it is delivered. As illustrated in Figure 2-5 (page 33), the range of CDS interventions is broad and extends far beyond rule-based approaches. While there are many successful examples of CDS interventions provided via paper-based systems, this book focuses on computer-facilitated interventions.

clinical decision support (CDS) program: consists of the overall set of CDS interventions that an organization uses to achieve its healthcare goals, as well as the processes used to select, prioritize, implement and evaluate these interventions.

clinical decision support (CDS) system: applications that deliver one or more CDS interventions.

clinical decision support (CDS) target: a specific, desired outcome intended from a CDS intervention.

clinical goal: more specific than a clinical decision support goal, it includes desired care processes or outcomes, such as reducing complications from diabetic kidney disease (see Figure 1-5, page 7).

clinical information systems (CIS): applications and hardware that manage patient care-related data.

clinical intervention: a specific patient care act (e.g., ordering or providing a diagnostic test or therapy).

clinical objectives: more specific and measurable components of clinical goals (e.g., increasing the rate of appropriate screening for diabetic kidney disease); see Figure 1-5, page 7.

clinical practice guideline: systematically developed statements to assist practitioners and patient decisions about appropriate healthcare for specific circumstances.[3]

coded data: individual data elements, such as a patient's medication or clinical problem, that are associated with a restricted set of defined terms; this restricted term set is often referred to as a controlled vocabulary.

Common Terminology Services (CTS): an HL7 standard for exchanging messages with a standard vocabulary in electronic format. Information systems can use the CTS standard, in combination with appropriate vocabularies, to translate from one code set to another and to look up a code given its name (and vice versa).

computer-based provider order entry (CPOE): allows prescribers/providers to enter orders directly into a computer rather than handwriting them. These systems are distinct from those that simply process orders entered by a third party (e.g., a nurse, pharmacist, or administrative clerk) and co-signed by physicians.

Consolidated Health Informatics (CHI): Cooperative venture by U.S. government agencies that deliver healthcare to establish standards and other means to foster interoperability of information systems (www.hhs.gov/healthit/chi.html).

content (clinical decision support): all forms of clinical information or knowledge that comprise the CDS interventions listed in Figure 2-5, page 33.

CPOE: see **computerized provider order entry**.

data warehouse: A centralized database system of clinical and administrative data drawn from multiple sources or other systems. In distinction to the clinical data repository (CDR), a data warehouse typically is structured to provide a view of data across multiple patients and encounters, does not collect data in real time, is employed for research and business purposes, and is not used directly in the delivery of clinical care. See also **clinical data repository**.

desired action: a patient care activity that will lead to achieving a specific clinical objective.

desired outcome: the positive results anticipated from implementing a particular clinical decision support intervention.

detractor: an individual who is vocal about his or her concerns about a clinical decision support intervention or the entire program and rather than working constructively with the team to address the concerns, actively works against it.

documentation template: a structured form for recording clinical information about a patient into a set of pre-defined data slots.

EHR: see **electronic health record**.

electronic health record (EHR): a collection of patient care data in electronic format along with the applications used to enter, view, and manipulate those data. Consisting of applications such as results review tools, laboratory and other ancillary information systems and computer-based provider order entry systems, the EHR may include the ability to look both at and across individual patients for purposes of financial management, decision support, outcomes reporting, resource planning, and public health.

electronic medical record (EMR): a single, secure application providing access to provider-entered clinical data used on a daily basis. It typically includes key health information and data such as a problem list, medication list, allergy list, notes, health maintenance information, and results retrieval (for laboratory, radiology, and other testing results) as well as provider communication and order entry. An EMR may be part of an overall electronic health record although this distinction is not universally accepted.

EMR: see **electronic medical record**.

expiration date (content): the last date that a particular clinical decision support feature will function (or be officially approved) unless it has been reviewed and reapproved by the appropriate oversight committee or individual.

free text: data entered into a field without any formal or pre-defined structure (such as would be provided by the use of a controlled vocabulary) other than the structure of natural language itself. Free text is the opposite of coded data.

functional testing: see **integration testing**.

functionality: describes the features or capabilities of a particular software application.

governance: the structure and processes whereby the strategy and direction of an organization are determined, implemented, and monitored.

guideline: see **clinical practice guideline**.

healthcare information technology (HIT): any computer-based equipment or system that is used to process data or information related to patient care.

Health Insurance Portability and Accountability Act of 1996 (HIPAA): a federal law in the U.S. that in part addresses healthcare information technology. The Administrative Simplification (AS) provisions of this Act are intended to reduce the costs and administrative burdens of healthcare by making possible the standardized, electronic transmission of many administrative and financial transactions. This Act also addresses the privacy and security of patient-specific healthcare information (www.hhs.gov/ocr/hipaa).

Healthcare Information and Management Systems Society (HIMSS): the healthcare industry's membership organization exclusively focused on providing leadership for the optimal use of healthcare information technology and management systems for the betterment of human health. HIMSS frames and leads healthcare public policy and industry practices through its advocacy, educational and professional development initiatives designed to promote information and management systems' contributions to ensuring quality patient care.

Health Level Seven (HL7): a standards-developing organization that provides standards (sometimes called specifications or protocols) for the exchange, management, and integration of data that support clinical patient care and the management, delivery, and evaluation of healthcare services (www.hl7.org).

health plan employer data and information set (HEDIS): a set of standardized performance measures, such as those addressing cancer and heart disease, designed to ensure that healthcare purchasers and consumers have the information they need to reliably compare the performance of managed healthcare plans. HEDIS is sponsored, supported, and maintained by National Committee for Quality Assurance (www.ncqa.org/Programs/HEDIS).

HEDIS: see **Health Plan Employer Data and Information Set**.

high-level clinical decision support (CDS) goal: strategic targets, such as increasing patient safety, that an organization might address with clinical decision support.

HIPAA: see **Health Insurance Portability and Accountability Act of 1996**.

HIS: see **hospital information system**.

HIT: see **healthcare information technology**.

HL7: see **Health Level Seven**.

implementation champion: see **champion**.

infobutton: an application that facilitates access to online clinical reference information from clinical information systems. Users of infobutton-enabled CIS can click a hyperlink or icon near a data element, such as a drug or clinical problem name, and retrieve reference information pertinent to that item.[4] Referred to in some organizations as KnowledgeLink.[5]

infrastructure (technology): refers to hardware and software available in the organization, including the clinical information systems, upon which clinical decision support interventions will depend.

Institute of Medicine (IOM): a component of the U.S. National Academy of Sciences that serves as an independent, scientific adviser to the nation to improve health (www.iom.edu).

integration testing: Ensures that all of the individually developed system components work as designed when integrated with the existing software systems. Also called functional testing.

IOM: see **Institute of Medicine**.

JCAHO: see **Joint Commission on Accreditation of Healthcare Organizations**.

Joint Commission on Accreditation of Healthcare Organizations (JCAHO): the principal accreditation body for hospitals and other healthcare delivery organizations in the U.S. It seeks to improve the safety and quality of care provided to the public through the provision of healthcare accreditation and related services that support performance improvement (www.jcaho.org).

knowledge assets: all or part of the collection of clinical decision support content available in a healthcare organization.

knowledge intervention: used synonymously with clinical decision support intervention in this book.

KnowledgeLink: see **infobutton**.

knowledge management: the processes whereby a healthcare organization acquires, uses, and maintains its clinical decision support knowledge assets.

launch: release of one or more clinical decision support interventions from development and testing into clinical use.

Leapfrog Group: an initiative driven by organizations that buy healthcare and that are working to initiate breakthrough improvements in the safety, quality, and affordability of healthcare for Americans. It is a voluntary program aimed at mobilizing employer purchasing power to alert America's health industry that big leaps in healthcare safety, quality, and customer value will be recognized and rewarded (www.leapfroggroup.org).

live testing: testing that occurs in the live, or production, clinical information system environment.

log file: a computer data file generated by a clinical information system or clinical decision support application that records information about the presentation of, and user response to, a clinical decision support intervention.

National Committee for Quality Assurance (NCQA): an independent, nonprofit organization with a mission to improve healthcare quality through measurement, transparency, and accountability. NCQA sponsors, supports, and maintains the HEDIS measures (www.ncqa.org).

National Quality Forum (NQF): a private, nonprofit membership organization created to improve healthcare in the U.S. through endorsement of consensus-based national standards for measurement and public reporting of healthcare performance data (www.qualityforum.org).

NQF: see **National Quality Forum**.

NCQA: see **National Committee for Quality Assurance**.

objective classes: a functional categorization of clinical objectives, designed to facilitate selection of CDS interventions. A given clinical objective can usually be identified as a member of one objective class; in turn, each class lends itself well to specific types of CDS interventions; see Figure 3-1 (page 43) and Figure 3-3 (page 46).

Office of the National Coordinator for Health Information Technology (ONCHIT): An office of the U.S. Department of Health and Human Services created to facilitate cooperation among government agencies, professional organizations, vendors and others in the deployment of information technology in healthcare (www.hhs.gov/healthit).

order set: a pre-defined and approved group of orders related to a particular clinical condition (e.g., hypertension treatment and monitoring) or stage of care (e.g., hospital admission to Coronary Care Unit). Often the order set consists of both diagnostic (i.e., laboratory tests or procedures) and therapeutic (i.e., medications or procedures) orders. The goals in creating order sets are to standardize care, increase compliance with best clinical practices, and facilitate the order entry process.

pay-for-performance programs: initiatives that more tightly couple provider reimbursement to measurable value in the process and outcomes of care.

performance improvement: the continuous monitoring and enhancement of healthcare processes and their outputs to increase the probability of achieving desired outcomes. Also refers to measurable progress toward achieving these outcomes.

personal health record (PHR): a secure, private application that enables a patient (or guardian) to review, create, or maintain healthcare-related documentation such as medications, medical problems, allergies, vaccination history, visit history, or communications with healthcare providers.[6]

PHR: see **personal health record**.

pilot launch: see **launch**.

quality assurance: systematic evaluation of an application or intervention to insure that it functions as intended and is problem-free.

quality measure: a feature or characteristic used to assess the quality of healthcare delivery. Quality measures are designed to provide meaningful information about whether care is safe, timely, effective, patient-centered, equitable, and efficient. For example, the percentage of patients with acute heart attack and no contraindications who receive aspirin within 24 hours before or after hospital arrival.

regression (verification) testing: selective testing of large software systems that have undergone modification; ensures that all new software is working as expected and that no new bugs have been introduced that could result in the failure of previously working functions.

reminder: see **alert**.

resistor: an individual affected by a clinical decision support intervention or program who resists his or her role in the clinical decision support implementation.

rollout: see **launch**.

shelf life (content): the expected time between launch of clinical decision support content and its expiration date. Unforeseen changes in clinical knowledge or changes in the availability of certain diagnostic tests, procedures, or medications can reduce the content's shelf life.

stakeholders: individuals, committees, and positions important for the success of individual clinical decision support interventions, or an entire clinical decision support program.

super users: clinical information system or clinical decision support users who are able to perform more functions and use the system more effectively and efficiently than average users.

system-initiated: interventions or actions that the clinical decision support application generates automatically without a request from a user. The opposite of user-initiated.

testing scenario: written description of a specific user interaction with a clinical decision support intervention and the expected results (based on a use case) that is used to ensure that the intervention about to be deployed will perform as designed.

unit testing: testing to ensure that the application has been built and functions as designed, independently of other parts of the overall system.

use cases/use case scenarios: step-by-step written descriptions of how users interact with an intervention, and the results of these interactions; typically based on the primary objective of the intervention (e.g., to respond appropriately when a drug is ordered to which the patient has a documented allergy).

user: an individual who is the recipient of a clinical decision support intervention.

user acceptance testing: pre-launch evaluation with intervention end-users to ensure that the intervention works as intended and is acceptable to them.

user-initiated: interventions or actions generated by the clinical information system or clinical decision support application in response to an explicit request in some form by a user. The opposite of system-initiated.

versioning: storing and managing successive versions of content, e.g., to provide details about the components of the content that were available at a given point in time.

workflow: the sequence of activities required of one or more participants in the healthcare delivery process (e.g., clinicians and patients) to accomplish a patient care task, or group of tasks.

References

1 Tang PC, Young CY. Active guidelines: integrating Web-based guidelines with computer-based patient records. *AMIA Proceedings.* 2000;843–7.

2 Kuperman GJ, et al. Detecting alerts, notifying the physician, and offering action items: a comprehensive alerting system. *AMIA Proceedings, Fall Symp.* 1996;704–8.

3 Field MJ, Lohr KN (eds). *Clinical Practice Guidelines: Directions for a New Program.* Institute of Medicine, Washington, DC: National Academy Press, 1990.

4 Cimino JJ, Elhanan G, Zeng Q. Supporting infobuttons with terminological knowledge. *AMIA Proceedings, Fall Symp.* 1997;528–32.

5 Maviglia S, Strasberg H, Bates D, Kuperman G. KnowledgeLink update: "just-in-time" context-sensitive drug information retrieval. *AMIA Proceedings.* Jan 2003:902.

6 Sittig DF. Personal health records on the internet: a snapshot of the pioneers at the end of the 20th Century. *Int J Med Inform.* 2002 Apr; 65(1):1–6.

Index

"f" next to page number denotes a Figure.